LEADERS ON ETHICS

Real-World Perspectives on Today's Business Challenges

Edited by John C. Knapp

Westport, Connecticut
London

Library of Congress Cataloging-in-Publication Data

Leaders on ethics : real-world perspectives on today's business challenges / Edited by John C. Knapp.

p.   cm.

Includes bibliographical references and index.

ISBN-13: 978–0–275–99671–0 (alk. paper)

1. Business ethics.   2. Social responsibility of business.   3. Leadership—Moral and ethical aspects.   4. Organizational behavior—Moral and ethical aspects.   5. Industrial management—Moral and ethical aspects.   I. Knapp, John C.

HF5387.L425   2007

174′.4—dc22   2007020613

British Library Cataloguing in Publication Data is available.

Library of Congress Catalog Card Number: 2007020613

ISBN-13: 978–0–275–99671–0

ISBN-10: 0–275–99671–9

First published in 2007

Praeger Publishers, 88 Post Road West, Westport, CT 06881

An imprint of Greenwood Publishing Group, Inc.

www.praeger.com

Printed in the United States of America

The paper used in this book complies with the Permanent Paper Standard issued by the National Information Standards Organization (Z39.48–1984).

10 9 8 7 6 5 4 3 2 1

Contents

Preface   vii

Introduction   ix

PART I: The Changing Role of Business in Society   1

 1 Crisis as a Platform for Change: Lessons from Coke and Corporate
America   3
Deval L. Patrick

 2 Unenlightened Self-Interest: The Wrong Response to Market
Capitalism   12
Daniel Yankelovich

 3 Restoring Corporate Trust: The New Imperative for Ethics,
Integrity, and Diversity   19
John F. Ward

 4 Ethical Governance and the Future of Free Enterprise   26
Steve Odland

 5 What Can the World's Religions Tell Us about Ethics in Business?   35
Edward Zinbarg

PART II: Ethical Concerns of Industry Sectors and Other Fields   41

 6 The Ethical Crises in the Accounting and Auditing Profession   43
James E. Copeland, Jr.

 7 Integrity and Profits: Can Companies Have Both in a World Where
Sex Sells?   51
Debra S. Waller

  8   The Moral Basis of Competitiveness   55
       Karen Katen

  9   Excellence without a Soul? Higher Education and the Shaping of
       Moral Character   64
       Harry R. Lewis

PART III: Leadership and Ethics in Organizations   71

 10   Building Trust in Trying Times   73
       Gerald Grinstein

 11   Delivering on Diversity Leadership: A Walk in the Other Guy's
       Shoes   80
       Cal Darden

 12   Leading with Values   86
       Charles M. Brewer

 13   Have You Hugged a Teamster Lately?   97
       Robert J. Rutland

 14   Leadership Challenges of Building a Company in Today's
       Environment   103
       John Wieland

 15   Ethics First: A Reform Agenda for City Government   107
       Shirley Franklin

Index   111

About the Editor and Contributors   115

Preface

A decade before the scandals at Enron and WorldCom made headlines, a group of Atlanta business leaders recognized that they had much to learn from one another about meeting the ethical challenges they often encountered in their work. And so began a series of gatherings where leaders shared common concerns and the lessons of their experience. From its inception as a discussion forum in 1993, this grassroots initiative grew to become one of the nation's leading centers of education for leaders seeking to strengthen ethics in business and society, The Southern Institute for Business and Professional Ethics.

Over the years, thousands of business men and women, professionals, and concerned citizens have participated in the institute's forums, roundtable dialogues, debates, and topical seminars, always in a spirit of mutual learning and respect. They have addressed an astonishing array of issues: environmental sustainability; product safety; truth in advertising; fraud prevention; racial discrimination; globalization; human rights; executive compensation; affordable housing; fair pricing; religion in the workplace; corporate social responsibility; youth character development; privacy protection; responsible governance; government corruption; transparency in international trade; child labor; hiring practices; values-based management; predatory lending; civility in politics; labor relations; journalism ethics; responsibilities of higher education; diversity management; bankruptcy; worker safety; and many others.

The book you are now holding is a product of their experience. Reprinted here are fifteen of the most thought-provoking speeches given by leaders to their peers. These exemplary presentations showcase corporate and public leaders in action, using public oratory to articulate values, voice positions on critical issues, share formative experiences, and exhort others to act. Most were transcribed from audio recordings and lightly edited to preserve the vitality of their living voices. All are printed here with the speakers' permission. Regrettably, space does not permit the inclusion of the lively discussions that followed these talks.

In these chapters you will encounter a diverse group of leaders in a variety of business and professional fields, from manufacturing and transportation to accounting and higher education. Though many of the issues they touch on are timeless, these speeches also capture moments in time, some recent, others more distant. The commentary in the introduction helps place the presentations in their proper historical contexts.

As you read these leaders' words, it is likely that you—like those who first heard them—will be inspired, informed, persuaded and, should you find yourself disagreeing with a point or two, even a bit exasperated. And that is how the speakers would wish it, for what is a speech without an audience's response? You will also find that the spoken word reveals the unique style and personality of each speaker.

It is significant that each of these leaders relied entirely on the spoken word to convey an important message—an old-fashioned but refreshing approach in this era of computer-based slide shows and special effects. Thus, they stand in a long tradition of orators who have used their own voices to give shape and substance to our understanding of ethics in public life.

The publication of this volume marks an important moment in the life of The Southern Institute for Business and Professional Ethics. In 2007, the nonprofit organization accepted an invitation to become a part of Georgia State University's J. Mack Robinson College of Business, one of the largest business schools in the United States. In this new home, the institute has embraced a broader mission of outreach, research, and teaching to promote ethics and global corporate responsibility. It also has expanded its unique programs of peer-to-peer learning in the business and professional communities, continuing the long-standing practice of encouraging open dialogue among leaders.

It is a privilege to express my sincere thanks to the countless individuals and organizations that have made The Southern Institute a vibrant center of thought leadership for fifteen years. In particular, I wish to acknowledge the many leaders—from speakers to volunteers to board members—who have made common cause for the betterment of business and society.

Introduction

When should leaders talk about ethics? In many businesses and other organizations, the subject is raised only in the aftermath of an ethical failure, a point when conversations turn to the unpleasant business of assigning (or avoiding) blame, making rules to prevent a recurrence of the problem, and controlling damage to relationships and reputation. A few years ago, this was the pattern of conversation in boardrooms, newsrooms, courtrooms, and Congressional hearing rooms in the wake of the corporate accounting scandals that shook worldwide confidence in American business.

It is still a familiar pattern in many organizations. An officer of a major public company recently told me of a planning meeting for her firm's global sales conference. "At one point," she recalled, "I suggested we include a session on ethics. All at once the room grew quiet. There was an awkward pause and then the conversation resumed as if I hadn't said a thing. I took that as a signal not to press the idea further." That might have been the end of it; but soon afterward she encountered the company's CEO in the lobby and took the opportunity to share her idea with him. To her surprise and disappointment, his reaction was as cool as the planning committee's. "The problem," he hastened to explain, "is that ethics is such a negative subject. The sales conference should be about motivating people, showcasing product innovations, and rolling out the new incentive plan. There's a time and a place for everything." Turning to walk away, he paused and asked, "Do you know of some ethical problem in the sales organization?" When she said she did not, the matter was dropped and never raised again.

SPEAKING OF ETHICS

This CEO is probably like many other leaders whose conversations about ethics have been mostly of the negative kind. If there is no immediate problem, they think it best not to raise an off-putting subject for which there is rarely a comfortable "time and place."

If leaders are reluctant to talk about ethics within their own organizations, how much more difficult must it be for them to speak *publicly* on the subject? As the U.S. Congress was passing the 2002 Sarbanes-Oxley reforms, a *Wall Street Journal* columnist asked why business leaders seemed so reluctant to speak out about the problems that had so severely damaged public confidence in American business. "The 'few bad apples' explanation for the current accountability crisis would be easier to accept if the public were hearing more from the 'good apples,' " wrote columnist Allan Murray. "But those apples are acting more like potatoes, buried further from public view. . . . " He speculated that many were "lying low and waiting for the storm to pass," possibly for fear of appearing sanctimonious or inviting scrutiny of their own glass houses.[1]

This muteness is puzzling. A McKinsey & Company survey in 2007 found that nearly half of U.S. executives agreed that they should play a leadership role in shaping public debate about social and political issues, yet only 14 percent said they actually do so. Of those who do speak publicly about issues, most said they were motivated by personal rather than business reasons.[2]

Yet speaking constructively to difficult issues is the very essence of good leadership, especially in this era of hyper-accountability, global information pipelines, 24-hour news cycles, and heightened public expectations for responsiveness and transparency. Critics increasingly call upon leaders of major institutions to address issues and answer questions in public. Indeed, Ronald Heifetz, founder of Harvard's Center for Public Leadership, argues that leadership becomes *most* "necessary to businesses and communities when people have tough challenges to tackle, when they have to change their ways in order to thrive or survive, when . . . current structures, procedures and processes will not longer suffice." These "adaptive challenges" typically arise when "a gap between aspiration and reality . . . demands a response outside the current repertoire."[3]

Ethical issues often bring attention to that gap, as the most difficult challenges outstrip our technical solutions, compliance measures, or legislative prescriptions. They call for leaders to describe problems clearly and realistically, choose between competing goods, and articulate new directions. One cannot do this with a closed mouth.

Leadership psychologist Howard Gardner argues that effective leaders "attempt to communicate, and to convince others, of a particular view, a clear vision of life."[4] They do so with speech backed by action, "through the stories or messages they communicate, and through the traits that they embody."[5] The test is simple but not always easy: Walk your talk.

Gardner says leaders tell stories of three types: Stories about self, stories about the group, and stories about values and meaning, all of which respond to a human need to make sense of life and its challenges.[6] If we apply Gardner's taxonomy to the speeches published here, we find that each of them embodies at least one type. For example: Two very different entrepreneurs, speaking at turning points in their careers, reflect on their personal experiences in leadership. Two more argue for the value of making diversity and inclusion higher priorities in business. A retired financial executive urges us to appreciate and use the ethical teachings of religions from disparate cultures. Three corporate executives respond to social concerns about their companies' roles in society. And the leaders of two preeminent institutions issue sober warnings about the future of their professions.

"Ethics talk" requires special competencies. With its roots in philosophical and religious traditions, the language of ethics can sound alien amidst the everyday parlance of business or other fields of practice. This requires leaders to forge a language to express values and beliefs in ways that resonate with practical concerns. What's more, without a good measure of self-awareness and humility, ethics talk can very easily lapse into self-righteousness.

Today's corporate leaders have new incentives to develop these competencies. A by-product of the corporate accounting scandals is a fresh emphasis on the responsibility of corporate leaders for setting an ethical "tone at the top" of their organizations. This phrase has even become a mantra for regulatory agencies and prosecutors, who discovered that the culprits in a number of the high-profile criminal cases were "C-level" executives, not rogue employees at lower levels. The Public Company Accounting Oversight Board, created by the Sarbanes-Oxley legislation, now audits accounting firms to determine if their executives are creating the correct "tone at the top." The director of enforcement for the U.S. Securities and Exchange Commission advises, "Whenever your CEO is delivering a state-of-the-company address to company employees, or offering remarks at a company event, she should be talking about the company's values as well as its profits." He adds that "the talk should extend beyond your company's own walls."[7]

PUBLIC ORATORY AS PERSUASION

If many leaders have for too long eschewed public discussion of ethics, others feel compelled to speak out. They call our attention to problems that must be remedied. They advocate new ways of living and leading. They reframe our views of issues and enable us to see them differently. Nearly always, they aim to persuade.

Gardner's ideas about leadership communication echo back to Aristotle's three elements of persuasion: *ethos*, *logos*, and *pathos*. *Ethos* refers to the character of the person doing the persuading. Does the leader have a reputation for credibility? Does the audience perceive a consistency between the leader's words and actions? *Logos* recognizes the necessity of logical, well-reasoned arguments. Does the leader offer persuasive facts to support her point of view? Does she demonstrate the knowledge and expertise to be regarded as an authority on the subject? *Pathos* underscores the power of emotional appeal. Does the leader speak to the heart as well as the mind?

In many of the chapters that follow, you will find all the elements of Aristotle's "art of persuasion," as well as examples of Gardner's story-telling method that draws from leaders' own experiences and sheds light on their personal character.

In these ways, each speech can be viewed as an act of leadership, an attempt to achieve something of importance through the art of persuasion.

Part I comprises four speeches addressing business issues in the larger, sometimes global, realm of society. We begin with Deval Patrick, a senior executive of The Coca-Cola Company, who cites some of his own company's challenges as examples of how crises can be catalysts to help businesses become more responsive to the needs of society. "When charges are leveled, global companies must not presume that the charges are false," he says, "not because global companies are inherently bad, but because in any large organization you can't know everything." Soon after this speech, he left the company to begin a successful campaign for Governor of Massachusetts. His remarks lead naturally to those of Daniel Yankelovich, a leading authority on social trends for more than four decades. In Chapter Two he describes a growing, worldwide demand for corporate accountability, but worries that many executives continue to make the mistake of focusing on short-term earnings at the expense of other responsibilities. "No business doctrine has raised a more impenetrable ethical fog than this perverted notion of shareholder value," he tells us. Yet he foresees a change for the better: "As [the fog] recedes, we will see an upgrading of the doctrine of corporate social responsibility."

Chapter Three features a timely perspective from Jack Ward, chairman and CEO of athletic goods producer Russell Corporation. Speaking in mid-2002, just weeks after the passage of the Sarbanes-Oxley legislation, he sees a silver lining in the cloud of scandal that has cast a shadow of distrust over corporate America. "That means the pressures on CEOs are even greater, but there has never been a better time for a CEO with ethics and values. These characteristics are being respected again. Making money the old-fashioned way is back in vogue. Two years ago you were considered a dinosaur if you didn't have fancy off-balance-sheet gimmicks or even if you manufactured something."

Turning a page to Chapter Four, we fast-forward four years to hear Steve Odland reflect on the magnitude of change that actually resulted from Sarbanes-Oxley and other reform measures. As chairman and CEO of Office Depot and head of Business Roundtable's task force on corporate governance, he enumerates a series of positive improvements, but sounds a warning: "Unfortunately, for some people the changes and the dramatic improvement in corporate governance have only spelled an appetite for more change, and the problem is that at some point you've got to stop changing; you've got to start letting things settle out. What we are worried about is that the new changes may fall victim to unintended consequences; that in addition to trying to fix what's wrong, we could break what's right."

This section concludes with a very different sort of speech. Ed Zinbarg is a former senior executive with Prudential Insurance Company who in retirement produced a well-researched book, *Faith, Morals and Money: What the World's Religions Tell Us about Ethics in the Marketplace*. Speaking as a businessman and noted economist, he explains, "I am a strong believer in the social progress that comes with a vigorously competitive marketplace that rewards efficiency and effectiveness. But there must be boundaries between competing vigorously and being a scoundrel. Where those boundaries lie is the big question." He shows that this question may be answered by studying the great religious traditions' teachings on vocation and commerce. He also argues that religious literacy is more important than ever in an increasingly globalized society—an insight he came by even before the events of September 11, 2001, made this apparent to many of the rest of us.

The speeches in Part II focus less on the larger marketplace than on the ethical challenges facing specific industries, professions, or sectors. James E. Copeland, retired chairman and CEO of Deloitte & Touche, delivers an incisive analysis of the "devastating" effects of ethical failures in the accounting and audit profession, and voices his doubts about the survival of the Big Four firms. He attributes the accounting crisis to a more pervasive ethical breakdown in society, which he calls a "global pandemic." "As we sift through the financial and human wreckage in our society, searching for clues to what went wrong, the only common denominator seems to be unethical behavior and a lack of character and integrity."

If it is true that moral standards in society are eroding, to what extent is business part of the problem? In Chapter Seven, Debra Waller, chairman and CEO of Jockey International, voices concerns about her industry's use of sexual imagery in advertising. "Because I'm in the underwear business, people sometimes ask me, 'So Debra is it true? Does sex really sell?' Of course the answer to this question is obvious. Yes sex does sell." Yet she contends that her company's refusal to follow this approach has become a positive differentiator of the Jockey brand.

In the next speech, a leader in a very different industry takes the podium to address an array of issues raised by critics. Karen Katen is vice chairman of Pfizer and president of Pfizer Human Health, the world's largest pharmaceutical company, which she tells us is in the "crosshairs" of health and money. "People deserve the first and earn the second—so they consider both of them rights. That's their starting point, and they find the concept of having to pay for a right morally problematic." She delivers a spirited defense of her company and industry, explaining the financial risks involved in developing new medications. "We should be looking not at cost but at cost-effectiveness," she says. "We should be looking at the value of health and the cost of disease, not just the price of medicines." The real moral question, she argues, is "how to get good health results."

Where Chapter Eight features a leader rising to the defense of her field, the next speaker has the opposite objective. Harry Lewis, professor and former dean of Harvard College, presents a serious-minded critique of his own institution and of higher education in general, which he believes have forgotten their most important mission. "We owe it to society to see that the future business leaders, government leaders, lawyers and doctors and teachers we produce will learn that their role in life is about something bigger than themselves and their personal success. Or at least, if they have the good fortune to have learned those values at home, we should not unteach them during the years they are in our care. If we don't do that job, then we should be held accountable for the white-collar crimes, the political corruptions, and the corporate scandals in which our graduates get involved."

Part III presents first-hand accounts of leadership within organizations. Few businesses have faced greater "adaptive challenges" than the commercial airlines in the period following September 11, 2001. When Delta Air Lines Chairman and CEO Gerald Grinstein spoke in April of 2005, fuel prices were climbing to new levels and his company was in crisis. Just five months later, Delta filed for Chapter 11 bankruptcy protection and joined three other major carriers in similar circumstances. Therefore, he chooses to speak at a crucial time in the life of his company. Although he addresses a range of complex business issues, at the heart of his remarks is a deep concern for restoring employees' trust in management. "I'm going to talk somewhat candidly about this," he tells his audience of business and community leaders. "We've had some difficult times in that respect, as you have seen in the press, and it has affected the company."

Turning to the next chapter, we listen as the head of U.S. operations for United Parcel Service shares a novel approach for helping high-potential managers develop greater compassion and sensitivity to others. Cal Darden, who at the time was among *Fortune* magazine's top ten "Most Powerful Black Executives in America," describes an executive internship program that sends fifty people a year to perform hands-on public service while living for a month in "communities afflicted with poverty, homelessness, spousal abuse, drugs, crime, and gang warfare." Speaking to diversity officers of more than forty major companies, he says the program results in greater empathy, a less-rigid style of management, and improved employee relations.

UPS is one of the world's largest employers with a reputation for a well-defined culture. By contrast, the speaker in Chapter Twelve is an entrepreneur who inspires us with a story of starting a business in his apartment and growing it into the second-largest Internet service provider. Charles Brewer's unconventional presentation (he even sings a song for the audience) matches the management style he became famous for as CEO of MindSpring Enterprises. Speaking after leaving the company to launch another new business, he shares some lessons from his experience developing a values-based approach to management. "For me, the core values and beliefs really were the whole point of the business, which was to change the way the world does business. I didn't really care if MindSpring was an Internet service provider or a cheese manufacturer." He encourages others to see their customers and employees in a new light: "Most individuals really want to accomplish something wonderful and meaningful with their work, and they are willing to work hard to make that happen. But somehow the organizations they work for make that difficult or impossible, and that's a real tragedy."

Robert J. Rutland leads a different kind of business, but is no less serious about instilling core values as the foundation of good employee relations. Allied Holdings is the world's largest transporter of automobiles, each month moving about one million new cars from manufacturers to dealers. A publicly held firm, most of its employees belong to the International Brotherhood of Teamsters. "As we tried to develop a strategy to run the company by love, care and hope, we had to be conscious of the type of business we were in, which was a diverse workforce of people who were away from us for most of their working careers," he explains. The solution he describes is a company-wide chaplaincy serving as a "ministry of presence" at every operating location in North America. "We have had strikes," he admits, "but our chaplains have continued to minister to the people, not taking a position on the issues." The result, he says, is the lowest employee turnover and best performance in the industry.

A third presentation on values-based leadership is given by one of the nation's most successful residential builders and developers. John Wieland, whose company has built more than 25,000 homes across the Southeast, reflects on three decades of experience as an entrepreneur in a difficult field. He concludes that a reputation for integrity is the critical success factor for business and thus requires the constant, personal attention of leadership. "One thing I've learned is that when your integrity is challenged, you need to handle that at the top." But this may be easier said than done, for he notes that although integrity is the "most important core value that appears in almost every company's list of core values," failure to take it seriously is "a great tragedy for American business."

We end with a speech by Shirley Franklin, elected mayor of Atlanta while her predecessor was facing a federal investigation for corruption. Shortly after taking office, she addresses community leaders to outline her plans for restoring public confidence in city government. It is a practical, step-by-step blueprint for strengthening compliance and ethics in the management of city hall. "We expect to make great progress in changing the culture of government and our ethics initiative is the cornerstone of this change," she says. "I will not tell you that it is easy. I won't tell you it is automatic." By the time she was elected to a second term in 2005, her "Ethics First" approach had been lauded with national awards for ethical leadership and recognition as *Governing* magazine's 2004 Public Official of the Year.

As you turn the pages of this book, you might imagine yourself in the audience of business leaders and concerned citizens where these speeches were first presented. Perhaps you, too, will be challenged or inspired to think in new ways about some of the most pressing issues of our time.

NOTES

1. Allan Murray, "CEOs Need to Speak out Amid the Corporate Crisis," *The Wall Street Journal*, August 6, 2002 (accessed online at www.wsj.com).

2. "CEOs as Public Leaders," *The McKinsey Quarterly*, December 2006 (accessed online at www.mckinsey.com).

3. Ronald A. Heifetz, "Anchoring Leadership in the Work of Adaptive Progress," in Frances Hesselbein and Marshall Goldsmith, eds., *The Leader of the Future* (San Francisco: Jossey-Bass, 2006), 73–77.

4. Howard Gardner, *Leading Minds: An Anatomy of Leadership* (New York: Basic Books, 1995), 42.

    5. Ibid., 37.

    6. Ibid., 50.

    7. "Tone at the Top: Getting It Right," remarks by Stephen M. Cutler, director of the
Division of Enforcement, U.S. Securities and Exchange Commission, at the Second Annual
General Counsel Roundtable, Washington, DC, December 3, 2004.

PART I

The Changing Role of Business in Society

Crisis as a Platform for Change: Lessons from Coke and Corporate America

Deval L. Patrick
*Executive Vice President, General Counsel and Corporate Secretary,
The Coca-Cola Company*
October 22, 2004

> For businesses trying to succeed globally, it is becoming harder to avert our eyes from people crushed by poverty or human rights abuses. Or to diminish the significance of the predictable human errors or oversights that arise in the running of any business.

Citizenship is an old-fashioned notion nowadays. And yet it expresses a very contemporary yearning, to see people in positions of power act responsibly—to see them put their civic duty first.

Business people are not immune from this yearning. Indeed, business today often requires going beyond adding value to the bottom line. It requires adding values to the way we do business. Some call this social responsibility. I call it simply good business.

The new globalized world market is making good business the only way to succeed in business today. When I began my career more than twenty-five years ago, globalization was a vague and distant image, the dawning of a day no one could quite yet make out. Back then, in the late 1970s, I was a very green emissary for a U.N. development project, traveling by camel, by foot, and on top of crowded cargo lorries in southern Egypt and the Sudan.

On one of my sojourns I had reached a small town out near the Chadi border, in the Darfur region you've been reading about recently, five hundred miles across the Nubian Desert through tracks in the sand. I found myself in a conversation with a local innkeeper. He told me that he had heard, years before, about a civil rights movement in America. "What happened to it?" he asked me bluntly. "Who won?"

Contrast that with former Treasury Secretary Larry Summers' story about an official trip to another part of Africa just a few years ago. He recalls riding in a dugout canoe when another man turned around with a cell phone in his hand and said, "Mr. Secretary, it's Washington on the line."

Globalization is here, and it represents one of the most profound transforma-
tions in human history. It describes a shifting landscape, an open world, enabled
by the fall of the Berlin Wall, the emergence of more open markets, and a sili-
con web that now connects Washington, DC, to a dugout in Africa, or Shanghai
to Palo Alto and Munich. So much of the world is connected by wire or satel-
lite today that now the affairs of distant nations are almost as immediate and
intimate as our own. Now your business anywhere is everybody's business everywhere. And because it is such a compelling idea and people can know more
about it than they ever could before, democracy itself has been catching on and
spreading.

For much of the world's people, globalization means steady, fulfilling work,
reasonable wages, more abundant and cheaper goods, and levels of wealth unimag-
inable two decades ago. It allows countries blessed in natural resources, whether
petroleum or coffee beans, to gain access to reliable markets on the other side of
the planet. It allows countries blessed in intellectual resources, like Ireland and
India, with their emphasis on education and proficiency in English, to sell their
services on the World Wide Web. Secretary Summers says that thanks to globalization, more than one quarter of humanity now enjoys growth at rates at which
living standards will quadruple within a generation.

And yet, there is a growing objection to slapping an "Open for Business" sign
across the entire planet. Some fear that unbridled free markets will destroy the very
natural ecosystems that sustain us. Others rebel against what one commentator
calls market fundamentalism—that unyielding belief that, despite its occasionally
severe swings, the market always gets it just right. Still others object to globalization because it threatens to overwhelm indigenous cultures by homogenizing (by
which I think they mean "Americanizing") their own cultures.

What if it turns out that globalization subjects all of us to faceless forces
unaccountable for any of the considerable human suffering still prevalent across the
world? As many as two billion people may be added to the world population over
the next twenty-five years—mostly in developing countries, and mostly in cities.
That's like adding to the planet, in a single generation, two hundred cities the size of
the greater Chicago area, where I grew up. Imagine that—two hundred Chicagos
in one generation. How will most of these people live? Today, as advanced as
our society is, two billion of our fellow human beings still don't have access to
electricity. Yes, I am connected to London and Shanghai and Sydney, but not to
Harlem or East Palo Alto or any of Rio's favellas.

More than one billion people live on a dollar a day. HIV and AIDS are on the
brink of wiping out an entire generation in sub-Saharan Africa. And some have
observed that just as good ideas like democracy proliferate in a globalized world,
so do bad ones, like terrorism. Hunger, disease, and despair are grinding daily
realities in many places abroad and at home. What does globalization offer them?
With globalization, many governments, including our own from time to time, have
withdrawn from addressing social needs, reducing themselves at their theoretical
extreme to mere market enablers.

A rising cadre of advocacy organizations—themselves global in scope, informed, organized, and politically savvy—compels us to pay more attention to social concerns. Some work in partnership with companies trying to feel their way through uncertain territory to what "good business" means today. Others are more confrontational. All are playing a role in making a new market with new rules and new expectations. For businesses trying to succeed globally it is becoming harder to avert our eyes from people crushed by poverty or human rights abuses, or to diminish the significance of the predictable human errors or oversights that arise in the running of any business.

We cannot avert our eyes because the media won't let us. The Internet won't let us. Our own people in the field won't let us. In an ironic way, globalization itself won't let us. As a very real result, a company's civic responsibility, its success at "good business," as I've described it, is becoming the price of entry into the global marketplace. None of us know yet fully what that means, because the rules are often unclear and conflicting. There are sovereign laws and government expectations. There are overlapping and sometimes conflicting demands of advocates. There are corporate codes of conduct that vary from company to company. And there is the complicating fact that for a global company like Coca-Cola, you must respect and respond to scores of different laws, codes, and guidelines simultaneously.

But the confusion that comes from all these competing agendas does not defeat the value of trying to come together on a few clear principles.

For years it was believed that business faced a stark tradeoff between shareholder value and social responsibility, between doing well and doing good. We are learning that this was a false choice all along. In today's world the right thing to do is more often also the prudent business choice. After all, there is no shareholder value in boycotts or sanctions over an accusation of human rights abuses in the workplace, no shareholder value in the inefficient use of natural resources. On the other hand, there is shareholder value in being known as a responsible partner to governments. There is shareholder value in being an environmental steward. There is value in living up to and surpassing the expectations of customers, business partners, employees, and neighbors in the communities where we operate. All of these are factors in investment decisions today, and I believe their significance will increase.

This is the context for discussion about lessons businesses might learn from companies in litigation crisis. It's important to consider litigation crises in the context of globalized commerce, because globalization has changed the definition of crisis. Information today, whether or not accurate, and opinion, whether or not informed, is everywhere. Like I said, today our business anywhere is everybody's business everywhere. A global footprint is a key characteristic, I think, in plaintiffs' counsel and enforcement agencies' consideration of how to target so-called impact cases—the kinds that create litigation crises. By impact cases, I mean cases with the broadest possible sweep, likely to generate the maximum attention.

The thinking is that public attention on the behaviors of companies with well-known brands and large workforces is not only a sort of "sweet spot," but it is also likely to cause a ripple effect on medium- and smaller-sized companies, thereby promoting greater compliance. That's why we see cases at large employers involving twenty to thirty thousand or more workers. Texaco, Mitsubishi, and our own Coca-Cola are examples of this. None of the issues in any of these celebrated discrimination lawsuits, for example, were especially unique—not one. In some cases, the issues, though real, are not as big as the press makes them out to be. But in the view of the enforcement agencies and the class action plaintiffs, making these kinds of employers targets will get the maximum bang for the buck, because globalization has changed the definition of crisis.

I think there are at least four basic lessons for global businesses facing litigation crises—four simple principles that are easy to remember but hard to do in the heat of the moment. They are: get all the facts and stick to them; respect your adversary; learn to listen; and use crisis as a platform for change. Here's what I mean.

First of all: *Get all the facts and stick with them.* This sounds so obvious, but you'd be surprised how many companies launch their defense without first determining whether they have anything worth defending.

Imagine a large company with a well-known brand. This company has successfully marketed on this consumer trust for decades and has built a worldwide business network as a result. It's a good employer. Among other modern employment policies, it has a well-stated nondiscrimination policy posted prominently in its facilities. It even has an affirmative action policy printed in its recruitment materials. It has a couple of women in its senior management, but no racial or ethnic minorities. Occasionally its senior managers are questioned by employee groups or investors about the lack of minorities in management. But the CEO confidently repeats what he's been told: "We can't find them" or "We can't hold onto them when we do." That CEO knows that the marketplace for employees and for sales is changing, but he is convinced the company is ready. He has made abundantly clear his company's interest in having qualified minorities and women on the payroll. The company also offers diversity training on how people feel about differences in the workplace—part of its effort to improve both workplace climate and retention. Besides, the company's payments to resolve discrimination claims have remained relatively low over time, amounting really to nothing more than a sort of modest cost of doing business.

So when that company is sued for discrimination by a class of black employees, the CEO immediately, and understandably, denies the charge, trivializes the complaints, and rails against the opportunistic plaintiffs' lawyers who brought the case.

But imagine the company has a restless and even widely unhappy group of minority employees. They feel they can get into the company, but can't move up. There is no apparent way to learn of opportunities for advancement until they are already filled, and there is no evident way to know what skills to develop to prepare oneself for promotions that might arise in the future.

Imagine also that there is no means for employees to express their concerns or even ask questions about the likelihood or prerequisites for advancement. And while the minorities know that they share these frustrations with their white colleagues, they suspect that the impact falls especially hard on them. Then consider what the minorities see and don't see in their own workplace. They don't see anyone like them in or on the brink of entering senior management ranks. They see no one like them in any of the company's recruitment materials, with the sole exception of the materials that have been created specifically to recruit minorities. And they know that the only minorities that the company is apparently seeking are the few on the four or five campuses where the company has been recruiting for years. They see no one who looks like them in the company's advertising, and they don't understand why the product they helped make around the world is hardly ever available in the neighborhoods they frequent. Throw in the fact that every once in a while, when the minority employee goes to the bathroom, they read some racist graffiti on the wall.

That was Texaco. Before the tapes. Its CEO believed in good faith that his company was doing all it could. The company believed it was ready for the future, and that its formula for success in the past would produce success in the future. And then came the tapes—recordings of executives making racist references about employees in the workplace that were made available to the press and broadcast around the world. And the rest, as they say, is history, or rather historic—the largest settlement in a discrimination case in American history at that time, and a public relations nightmare that put the value of its name brand in jeopardy.

Leave aside the tapes and a few of the other sensational details, the experience was similar at the Coca-Cola Company just a few years later.

What is my point? When charges are leveled, global companies must not presume that the charges are false—not because global companies are inherently bad, but because in any large organization you can't know everything. Life in the vaulted quarters of the executive suite is very sweet. But it's also very, very isolated. If you sit in your office and limit your context to other executives, you frequently don't know all you need to know.

So, before leaders of big companies refute charges, they should take the time to get the facts. The press shop will always pressure you to refute the charges immediately and categorically, but in most cases that's a mistake. Take the time to find out reality, and then face that reality squarely. In all the books on successful leadership generally, and crisis management in particular, I can think of no example where anyone was able to spin their way to success.

Remember too, the context for my comments—this is a globalized world. Whatever is alleged—especially if it's sensational—and whatever companies respond is immediately distributed around the world. When the charges are disproved, the press never seems quite as broad as when the charges are first leveled. But when the company reflexively denies a charge that is ultimately borne out by facts, the lingering effect is especially damaging. Get the facts first and stick to them.

My second point: *Respect your adversary.* My grandfather swept the floors of a bank for forty-five years on the south side of Chicago where I grew up. And yet when he walked through that place he was treated like a dignitary. He wouldn't retire. They couldn't make him go home. When he died, the chairman of the bank spoke at his funeral and said that had it been a different time, my grandfather would probably have retired as chairman of that bank himself. His experience and others like it helped me fully appreciate and learn to see the dignity in every living soul. Respect for human dignity should compel respect for your adversary.

Sometimes charges raised stem from bruised feelings or some sense of personal unfairness unrelated to the cause of action that's stated. It's tempting to belittle the claimant, her lawyer, the legal system, or all three. But the claim is usually real to the claimant. Nothing antagonizes more than treating a complainant as if their concerns are trivial. That approach has prolonged more than a few lawsuits.

This is as true of government agencies as it is of the individuals who staff them. Several years ago, our company's and our bottlers' offices in Europe were raided by the European Commission antitrust authorities. Thousands of documents were seized as part of a wide-ranging investigation of our competitive practices throughout Europe. We were facing serious charges, a finding that would limit our ability to acquire businesses in Europe in the future, and fines that could range up to half a billion dollars.

Our team was in full battle mode when I arrived at the Coca-Cola Company in 2001. We were debating with the Commission their jurisdiction, the soundness of their legal theories, and even the competence of their staff. Indeed, we were arguing that EU interpretation of EU law was unsound because it was inconsistent with American interpretation of American law. And we had a legion of experts to help demonstrate how the EU's analytical approach was wrong. We had a scorched-earth strategy. In fact, we had several scorched-earth strategies, because each of the bottlers had a slightly different one and the Coca-Cola Company was largely absent.

Well, you can imagine that nothing conveyed disrespect to the Commission more than our lecturing them on the flaws in their interpretation of their own sovereign laws. It displayed a lack of respect for our adversary, and impatience, if not contempt, for the job they had to do. It also revealed how little we appreciated the importance to our business of having a successful ongoing relationship with the Commission after this dispute was over. So, we changed our strategy and we changed our team. We embarked on a course of reconciliation and cooperation. We rebuilt trust and respect in our relationship. And we settled the matter—in a way that clarified the rules under which we can successfully compete in Europe and without paying a single red cent in fines. Respect your adversary, and in my experience, your adversary will respect you. It's all about according others their dignity.

At the Coca-Cola Company, respect for individual human dignity is a core value. If we keep our people in the forefront, if we hold respect for their safety, health, and dignity as paramount, most other policies will fall into place. To that end, in our own and our bottlers' operations, we have policies that expressly reject child labor, involuntary servitude, or physical abuse; respect the freedom of association, including the right to organize; commit to fair compensation; and assure a safe and healthy work environment.

Now, devising such an internal standard is, frankly, the easy part. It's expected and in most cases, it's the law. We and many other companies go beyond the law in exercising direct influence over joint ventures, alliances, contractors, and vendors by insisting that they meet the company's internal standards, too.

This is becoming the norm for us, no less than for the big box retailers who learn to apply strict codes of conduct to apparel suppliers in the developing world. Our challenge may, in fact, be more complex, for we recognize that we must partner with, and contribute to, the economic and social development of the countries in which we operate, and in doing so, promote positive social change. Here we have to be realistic about our role and manage expectations of that role, for we are guests in our hosts' countries and a private company cannot deal with a sovereign government as an equal. We certainly cannot dictate social policies. But we can be a force for positive change wherever we do business—to be a responsible global citizen, as our former boss at Texaco used to say.

Let me add a point here about how we value diversity, because this relates directly, in my view, to human dignity. The Coca-Cola Company long had a commitment to diversity. But we learned the hard way that in order to make diversity work, if you always do what you always did, you'll always get what you always got. We learned that you can have all the directives imaginable and all the right intentions. But if you don't have a sustained, focused commitment from the top and a means to hold people accountable for workplace fairness, you will come up short every time. At Coca-Cola today, one factor in determining executive compensation is the ability to recruit, retain, and develop a diverse workforce. In a corporate culture where relationships with powerful allies determined your career advancement, we now use clear, relevant job competencies to assess new hires and candidates for promotion. As a result of leveling the playing field, in the United States, racial and ethnic minorities now make up 41 percent of new hires and women comprise about half. That is good news, because by drawing on the unique diversity of America, global companies like ours strengthen their competitive position around the world. We have work to do, but that is good news.

Number three: *Learn to listen*. It is a fundamental feature of human personality to want to be heard. Not just listened to, but heard. It is also widely assumed by skeptical American workers everywhere that large companies don't listen. So many litigation crises arise from the gap between those two.

In our own company early last year, an employee raised several concerns about accounting and other commercial practices in our fountain business. He spoke with his colleagues and his supervisor. He even tried to raise the issues with the president of the company. By the time he reached me he was on his way out of the company as a part of a large reduction in force. And by then he was convinced of two things: that his separation was the result of having raised the issues in the first place, and that the lawyers investigating were investigating in order to cover things up rather than to uncover the truth.

When Matthew Whitley's claims became public and the litigation began, we went into full battle mode, hurling hyperbole back and forth between the lawyers and questioning each other's motives. Meanwhile, our workforce was upset and embarrassed, the investor community was anxious, our relationship with a major customer was seriously jeopardized, and the U.S. Attorney and SEC came to call. As an interesting aside, it was not for a few months later, when Matt and I finally got a chance to sit down together, that I finally understood that while we were focusing on whether we had complied with the accounting rules, Matt was concerned with whether his discharge was fair. In a way, he and the company were talking right past each other.

But we learned to listen. We learned to appreciate Matt as a resource for our investigation, to pursue his issues seriously, to give him as much feedback as we could on what we found. And we learned from him that, although most of what he alleged was not substantiated by the facts, some of it was true and needed to be addressed. Indeed, in the course of the investigation we learned other things that we needed to know, and that we needed to address. The point is that we had to learn to listen to Matt, even though he was our adversary, and the cause of many a sleepless night in the early days. And once we did learn to listen to him we were able to find solutions. We settled his $44 million claim for $100,000 plus severance and fees. We dismissed a federal court action, a state court action, and a Department of Labor investigation. We repaired an important relationship with a customer and its franchisees, and we addressed certain weaknesses in our control mechanisms and our management that had gone unaddressed. Fortunately, none of the facts revealed any financially material concerns. But what we learned we needed to learn and we fixed. And I think the U.S. Attorney and the SEC are beginning to see that, too.

My point is simply this. Though the instinct in crisis is to build a moat, there is more value in building a bridge. Learn to listen.

Finally, I believe that *crisis can be a platform for change*. In some ways this is the action item that derives from the other lessons. Respecting your adversary. Getting and facing the facts squarely. Listening to the essence of the concerns being raised. All are essential prerequisites to meaningful change. Indeed, in some of the cases that I've mentioned, the crisis created the opportunity to accelerate changes already desired. At both Texaco and Coca-Cola, efforts to enhance workplace fairness and inclusion were already underway when the lawsuits were filed, but the resolution of those cases in each instance accelerated those efforts. Resources and outside expertise were added to existing capability to enhance success. In addition, in each case, concerns about the fairness of certain HR practices, like promotions or performance appraisals, were in fact shared by white employees, too, so that addressing the issues raised by minorities meant improving the work conditions for everybody.

At Coca-Cola, some of Matt Whitley's claims caused us to reexamine some of our control practices and make improvements. For example, our internal audit function now reports directly into headquarters from throughout the business operations. And we make a practice now of informing customers of any employee infraction of our code of business conduct that involves their account, an embarrassing oversight in the Burger King incident from which we learned a lesson. This lesson is probably, you know, nothing more than the sort of common sense of learning from one's mistakes. I mention it only because I think the resentment about being thrown into crisis, about being on the sharp end of that particular stick, sometimes obscures the value of the change urged upon us in the first place.

The lessons I've spoken of today are, I believe, the imperatives of working within a polyglot world. A world that is developed and developing, a world burdened with need and still trembling with hope—above all a world whose warts and blemishes, whether on individuals or companies, are more transparent than ever.

This brings me back to globalization. I agree with the observation of U.N. Secretary General Kofi Annan, who said that whatever cause you champion, the cure does not lie in protesting against globalization itself. The poor are not poor because of globalization, but because of too little globalization, because they are not part of it, because they are excluded.

There is a constructive role for global business in this revolution, even out of crisis. We have an implicit challenge to include the excluded, by respecting our people, our communities, even our adversaries; by learning to listen to anything without losing our temper or our self-confidence; by building better companies on the strength of what we learned. That challenge must be accepted, and it must be met.

CHAPTER TWO

Unenlightened Self-Interest: The Wrong Response to Market Capitalism

Daniel Yankelovich
Author and Founder of Viewpoint Learning and Public Agenda
January 11, 2007

> The pragmatic reality is that the invisible hand often needs a little help. If there is no automatic link between profitability and the public good, a link must be deliberately forged.

In the many decades I've been studying trends, I have never known a time like the present when so many trends are converging to reshape the business environment and to create a new stage of market capitalism.

Let me start by mentioning some of the trends that are transforming the economic world in which we live.

CHINDIA: Many more nations have become high-growth players in the global economy. The United States was once virtually the sole engine of international economic growth. But now India and China lead a plethora of countries in contributing to a steady global growth.

EXPORTING JOBS: An extraordinary global market for labor and talent exists today, creating an important new political issue around peoples' fear of "exporting American jobs."

NEW ENTRANTS: There are billions of people around the globe who are just beginning to enter the market economy, with as many as two billion now subsisting on less than $2 a day.

NEW SOCIAL EXPECTATIONS: An important set of trends revolves around new societal expectations of business, particularly the growing demand for environmental sustainability as a response to climate change. But new societal expectations are also driving greater transparency in companies and bringing pressure on them to participate in reducing world poverty.

MORE NGOs: Accompanying these new social expectations, the number of organized stakeholders has exploded. In the last decade alone, the number of non-governmental organizations (NGOs) in the world has expanded from 8,000 or so to more than 45,000 today.

CONNECTIVITY: On the technological side, universal connectivity helps to create a single more unified world market.

GROWING ENERGY DEMANDS: All this growth strains the global energy system, such that in the next fifty years energy demand will be two to three times as great as it has been in the past hundred years.

These and other trends are converging to shape a very different environment for business. They are putting particular stress on the ethical practices of companies, especially large international corporations. In recent years we have seen a number of great companies—not scandal-ridden companies like Enron, but solid reputable companies like Hewlett-Packard and Pfizer and AIG and Fannie Mae and Shell and Citigroup—who have had trouble in adapting their ethics to this swiftly changing world.

Over a long business life, I have served on more than a dozen boards and consulted with dozens of companies. This experience has left me with an image of an ethical hierarchy of companies in the shape of a pyramid. At the broad base of the pyramid are those companies that equate ethics simply with what is legal. The questions they ask are, "Is it legal?" and "Can we get away with it?"

The next level up the pyramid encompasses companies that do distinguish between the legal and the ethical. In these companies, even when some action may be deemed OK by their lawyers, at least one director will protest and say, "I don't care whether it's legal or not. Does it pass the 'smell test'?"

I greatly admire these independent directors, but pragmatically, the ethical concern at both levels is still essentially negative. Even those companies who insist that their actions pass the small test are more concerned with avoiding bad behavior than with doing positive good.

At the very apex of the triangle, we do find a smaller group of companies who are *actively* seeking a positive ethical goal. Their executives ask the question, "Can we do something good for the larger society? Can we serve the nation as well as make a profit?"

Now it is true that there is only a small group of companies at the apex. But they are part of a long tradition of market capitalism that traces back to Adam Smith in the eighteenth century. Adam Smith is best known today for a narrow Milton Friedman—conception of market capitalism that focuses solely on the bottom line. Friedman interpreted Smith's doctrine of the "invisible hand" as a guarantee that any company who makes a profit must by definition be doing good for the larger society. But Smith's version of capitalism was far deeper and broader, revolving around the concept of "enlightened self-interest."

Companies at the apex of the pyramid are searching for forms of enlightened self-interest suitable for the era in which we live. In my book, *Profit with Honor*, I argue that every era has to define for itself what enlightened self-interest means for that era, and that a return to the tradition of enlightened self-interest is a key requirement for success in this new stage of market capitalism.

The business scandals that have plagued our era are an expression of *un*enlightened self-interest. Their core ethical value has been *Winning for Yourself*—we win, you lose. Sad to say, the source of this degraded norm of winning for yourself is to be found in the evolution of our cultural values. Ever since the wave of new social values was introduced in the 1960s and 1970s, our society has grown more tolerant and pluralistic. These are positive accomplishments. But the new social values have also led to a number of less benign unintended consequences. They have promoted a strikingly self-centered form of individualism that encourages people to look out for themselves even at the expense of others. They have undermined the more traditional American values associated with enlightened self-interest.

If you look at the business scandals as an expression of the larger culture, they reveal that the ethical orientation of companies that cluster at the bottom of the pyramid gets them into business trouble as well as ethical/legal trouble. Their low ethical standards are doing untold damage to their companies' reputation for integrity and trustworthiness—what we call "trust equity." A company's trust equity can be a major competitive asset; the lack of it, a major liability. Trust equity is difficult to build and easy to lose. In these past decades, some of the world's most successful companies have taken serious hits to their trust equity—not the criminal behavior associated with the scandals but the simple loss of the trust essential to the long-tem success of corporations.

Many companies today resist accepting responsibilities beyond making a profit for their shareholders. They do not do so because of lack of personal ethics but because of their ideological belief in the doctrine of the "invisible hand"—the doctrine that the marketplace ensures that a company that is profitable *must* be serving the public good, irrespective of how that profit is made. And this belief is powerfully reinforced on Wall Street by the doctrine of shareholder value—the belief that if you give the shareholder priority, you automatically benefit all other stakeholders.

A McKinsey & Company survey last year showed that businesses worldwide are beginning to move away from this Milton Friedman conception of market capitalism. The McKinsey study found that an impressive 84 percent of business executives across the globe now believe that the role of business must be broader than the bottom line. This indicates an emerging norm in the international business community.

What is particularly interesting about the survey is that these same executives were self-critical of their own methods for achieving a broader engagement with the society. They felt they were using the wrong tools, such as lobbying, PR, advertising, various forms of spin and clever lawyering. (The former CEO of Pfizer was a leader in lobbying to keep Americans from importing lower cost drugs from Canada while at the same time appearing on Pfizer's advertising campaign as it touted itself as a caring company). Those spin tactics may seem to make sense within the company, but they are seen from the outside as the kind of hypocrisy that erodes a company's trust equity.

Executives in the McKinsey survey said they have to begin to move toward different tools—tools like transparency and engaging a wider range of stakeholders rather than just shareholders.

Let me try to forecast for you what I think is going to happen in the next decade or so, as business struggles to reconcile demands for a broader engagement beyond the bottom line with the practical realities and pressures from the investment community for short-term profitability. I believe that within the next five years one company after another will quietly abandon the concept of shareholder value that has been so prevalent on Wall Street. There is too much baggage associated with it, too much hypocrisy and perversion of the original concept. Remember that the original concept of shareholder value was focused on *long-term* profitability. But it has been transmuted to mean *short-term* profitability, which privileges one group of stakeholders—shareholders—over all others. Often the shareholder is visualized sentimentally as a little old lady or a genteel retired couple loyally holding onto their few shares, where in reality the typical shareholder is a thirty-two-year-old fund manager who couldn't care less about your stock and will dump it in a nano-second if your quarterly profits fall by pennies a share.

No business doctrine has raised a more impenetrable ethical fog than this perverted notion of shareholder value. As it recedes, we will see an upgrading of the doctrine of corporate social responsibility (CSR) that has evolved quite a bit since I first became familiar with it in the 1970s. In its earliest embodiments, CSR was often naïve. When IBM was still under Tom Watson's leadership, in the name of corporate social responsibility, Watson decided to create a school in New York's Harlem district and a training camp in Massachusetts for underprivileged young people. Watson spent more of his time worrying about these kids stealing the camp's equipment or playing hooky from the school than he did about the company's strategic planning! In those days, CSR insisted that companies do good things for the society in ways that were totally unrelated to the business. Nowadays, fortunately, the emphasis has been reversed.

Last year, the *Economist* magazine published a long piece fiercely critical of the corporate social responsibility movement. The *Economist* insisted that all corporate actions, including those taken in the name of corporate social responsibility, should be subject to two criteria:

• Does the action improve the company's long-term profitability?
• Does it advance the broader public good?

The *Economist* was criticizing CSR for stressing the second criterion (advancing the public good) at the expense of its profitability. But the very act of creating two criteria challenges the basic assumptions of the Milton Friedman/shareholder value ideology, which has just one criterion: Does a company action enhance corporate profitability? (The premise here is that anything that advances corporate profitability automatically advances the public good as well.) But once you apply the *Economist's* dual criteria, pragmatism rather than ideology becomes the norm. Pragmatism demonstrates what common sense would expect. Sometimes company profitability does contribute to the public good and sometimes it doesn't. Sometimes the two are linked but often they are not. That's one of the realities that the folks at GM failed to grasp when they ended up with the Hummer while Toyota created the hybrid. Enlightened self-interest for our era means that corporations have to apply the two criteria, and not blindly rely on outmoded dogma.

Let me give you a handful of examples of the sorts of things that some companies are doing to meet these two criteria.

Lee Scott, CEO of Wal-Mart, has been under enormous pressure to respond to demands for greater corporate responsibility. At one point he called Jeff Immelt, CEO of General Electric, and said that if G.E. could produce light bulbs that took less energy, Wal-Mart could sell a zillion of them. Also, in lowering its price for generic drugs, Wal-Mart has sought to advance the public good and made profits for itself at the same time.

General Electric has a program called Eco-magination that involves a huge investment in new technologies to solve global environmental problems. Immelt says explicitly, "We plan to make money doing it. Increasingly, green is green."

A few years ago, Proctor & Gamble introduced a low-priced water softener, called PUR, for developing countries. Initially it was unprofitable because even at its low price it was too expensive and too complicated to use for average buyers in poor nations. So P&G repriced it, redesigned it, and reintroduced it with a commitment by the company to offer it (profitably) to at least two developing countries a year for the next twelve years.

Unilever has introduced the single largest health program in India designed to get children to wash their hands to prevent a major source of diarrhea-associated problems. Unilever makes Lifebuoy, the most popular soap in India. This program meets both criteria—it advances the company's business interests and also an important public health objective.

At the other extreme, the most egregious example of poor stewardship and of ignoring the dual criteria may be the almost universal practice of hospitals that charge the uninsured more than the insured for the same medical services. Since the uninsured tend to be poorer, they are hounded into bankruptcy. Astonishingly, more than half of all the bankruptcies in the United States are related to illnesses and the inability to deal with their unanticipated high costs.

The pragmatic reality is that the invisible hand often needs a little help. If there is no automatic link between profitability and the public good, a link must be deliberately forged.

There are many different ways to do this. I want to mention one we are currently experimenting with. In the new global economy, one of any company's greatest challenges is to prevent being taken by surprise when the tectonic plates undergirding globalization shift in ways that the company had not anticipated. CEOs must always have at their fingertips a feel for how to take advantage of global change and certainly not be victimized by it. How best can they hone that responsiveness to change? Our solution has been to introduce a new function within the company that we call Strategic Dialogue.

The idea here is to form a new Strategic Dialogue unit in the company that reports either to the CEO or the board. In a large company the new unit probably involves about a dozen participants from various parts of the company; perhaps fewer in a smaller business. These would be among the most creative and thoughtful people irrespective of what parts of the company and what functions they represent.

The purpose of the new unit is to develop strategies for adapting to change. Specifically, the group should start with the new trends that are reshaping the global economy. It should then screen them to select among them the few trends that are most relevant to the company's future. This will involve identifying and analyzing a wide array of trends—not just demographics, but also technological, cultural, geopolitical, economic, and business trends.

Using dialogic methods the group will develop various scenarios for how the company can best respond to these trends in ways that are both profitable and also contribute to the public good. (Dialogic methods are necessary because when specialists encased within their own stovepipes work with others similarly encased, they become productive only when they are able to communicate across conflicting frameworks. The methods of formal dialogue are the only ones that permit people who do not share the same frameworks but who do share common interests to contribute to each other's thinking and work.)

In sum, the new stage of Market Capitalism calls for a redefinition of enlightened self-interest with less emphasis on what is merely legal or morally smelly, and more emphasis on what contributes actively to the public good. In this way, the bottom of the pyramid gets squashed down and the top is enlarged.

There are several business doctrines that can accelerate this trend. One involves a doctrine I call Stewardship Ethics, and develop in *Profit with Honor*. The core idea of stewardship is that you leave the organization of which you are the steward in better shape than when you started. The essence of stewardship has to do with *caring*, and particularly with caring for all constituents rather than just shareholders just employees.

I will close with a few thoughts on the role of education in the new stage of market capitalism. A number of years ago, The *Harvard Business Review* asked me to interview graduates of the class of '49—the most famous class that ever graduated from Harvard Business School. As we talked with these mostly retired executives about their early life it grew very clear that the ethics they had absorbed from their families was what carried them through their toughest challenges. Many of them confessed that they didn't always live up to the standards their parents had set, which they now regretted.

Today's win-for-yourself ethic in the larger culture makes it more difficult to pursue that same sort of ethical obligation. For the most part, business schools have scanted ethics. They have taught it as an afterthought or a course that need not be taken seriously.

The challenge for business schools today is to make central the point that I've been urging in this discussion—that rediscovering and redefining the doctrine of enlightened self-interest is the key to success in today's global economy. The business schools need to develop many more practical case histories of how companies strengthened their trust equity or undermined it, with what consequences. They need to show how Strategic Dialogue can be made to work to reconcile profitability with serving the public good.

Every successful executive will have to resolve the conflict between building trust equity through practices that represent enlightened self-interest versus the practice of maximizing short-term profitability without taking the public good into account and then rationalizing that somehow the public good is served as an automatic byproduct of this behavior. Business schools should help redefine enlightened self-interest for our era. In the end, the major test of a CEO's stewardship and integrity will be how well he or she cares for the company's various constituencies and balances their competing claims. That is the key to redefining enlightened self-interest for our times.

I believe this trend will prove robust. Every corporate boardroom struggles with this issue. If market capitalism is to evolve and to enhance the global economy, the one constant through all the tectonic changes of market capitalism is the idea of doing well by doing good.

CHAPTER THREE

Restoring Corporate Trust: The New Imperative for Ethics, Integrity, and Diversity

John F. Ward
Chairman and CEO, Russell Corporation
September 18, 2002

> We have to select and value CEOs that are ethical. Up until recently, however, we too often rewarded CEOs for results no matter how the game was played.

When John Knapp and I first talked about the possibility of my presenting to The Southern Institute for Business and Professional Ethics a number of months ago, corporate ethics was an issue but not the perceived crisis it is today. Recent research studies have indicated that the public believes that many CEOs are not ethical and that they leave their values at the door of the office in pursuit of the almighty dollar. Yet, we know of the 15,000 public companies, only a handful are creating this highly negative perception. However, the abuse that we have seen by those few companies goes beyond anything that I thought would or could occur, and it is creating a major mistrust of business.

Changes in how companies operate are necessary but we must remember not to punish the innocent in order to punish the guilty. As you have heard, my perspective on this subject is unique, having spent most of my career at large public corporations, but also having taught business ethics at Wake Forest University. By the way, I had never thought of teaching until I was approached by Wake Forest to teach ethics. This is one of the subjects that I feel passionate enough about to change my plans in order to teach it. Rather than teaching from a book, most of the case studies I used were true-life situations where names and even industries were changed to protect the innocent.

Over the past few months, I have both participated in and spoken at several conferences dealing with corporate ethics. We at Russell have personally been hurt by a major account receivable write-off at K-Mart where we gave credit based on financial reports that eventually had to be restated. Experience, mixed with personal belief, continues to reinforce to me that we must restore public confidence and trust in business. First, we must remember that no law or signed document can ensure ethical and legal behavior. Much of the behavior that created this crisis was already illegal, as demonstrated by the many arrests that have been made. In any field there will always be some people with criminal intent. We must take every step possible to ensure that these people do not get into public corporations, and if they do, that they are rapidly removed from their positions.

Yet, what can we really do to make sure that all companies operate in an ethical fashion? There is really only one way. We have to select and value CEOs that are ethical. Up until recently, however, we too often rewarded CEOs for results no matter how the game was played. Over the long run, ethical companies should win out, although, unfortunately, this is not always the case. And it won't be as long as Wall Street continues to reward only short-term results.

During my class, I talked about Al Dunlap, the ex-CEO of Sunbeam Corporation, and Aaron Feurestein, CEO of Malden Mills, the maker of Polar Fleece, as examples of philosophies I disagreed with and of values I respected. Al Dunlap was highly praised by Wall Street and rewarded for what he accomplished at Scott Paper. It was reported that he believed corporations should have only one stakeholder, the shareholder.

The Aaron Feurestein situation was the exact opposite. When fire burned down the Malden Mills plant, he kept paying the employees even though they weren't working. He rebuilt the plant and did everything possible to help the employees, even though it put the company at risk. The company survived the fire but, unfortunately, Malden Mills couldn't survive operating the way it was in the highly competitive global market place and went into Chapter 11 bankruptcy.

So, as we see, there must be a balance. As Marianne Jennings wrote in a recent article in the *Washington Post* entitled "Remember the Business in Business Ethics," you still need to make the right business decisions. You can't escape from the competitive environment and this eventually negatively impacted Malden Mills. Major retailers were able to sell quality products competitive to Polar Fleece at one half the price of Malden Mills' product. Malden Mills didn't move production to low-cost areas of the world and the company went into bankruptcy.

A leader has to make tough competitive decisions even when it negatively affects some employees. That means the pressures on CEOs are greater than ever, but there also has never been a better time for a CEO with ethics and values. These characteristics are being respected again. Making money the old-fashioned way is back in vogue. Two years ago you were considered a dinosaur if you didn't have fancy off-balance sheet gimmicks or even if you manufactured something. Companies like Russell, with our 100-year tradition of values, are now being appreciated again.

The most tremendous pressure on CEOs continues to be the need to make their numbers every quarter. Turnover of CEOs has increased 50 percent in the last few years and much of that is tied to whether or not they hit those numbers—every three months. In what other field do you get strongly punished for achieving

99 percent of your goal? But a 1 percent miss in earnings per share can result in up to a 20 percent decline in your stock price. Wall Street, and all of us as investors, must value ethics and long-term growth as well as short-term results. We are all involved because most of us have 401(k)s or pension funds and each month we open our statement to see where our stock prices are. We want to see the funds up. We want short-term results. So, unfortunately, unethical behavior has been rewarded in the past as long as the stock price was going up.

In the go-go market years, we have also seen boards of directors selecting CEOs based on their star value. Big names with big egos were hired and paid enormous packages. They were made to feel above the rules. In fact, Jim Collins in his top-selling book, *Good to Great*, states there is often a reverse correlation to a CEO's star value and long-term results. CEOs with big egos can make big mistakes. They can get caught up in their own hype.

I couldn't believe the comments from several of the top executives arrested for fraud or dipping into corporate funds for personal use. They denied their guilt and I am not sure they actually understood that what they were doing was wrong. They may have thought they were above the law, that these public companies were really their own personal businesses.

Boards must put a greater emphasis on choosing the right leaders and business ethics must be at the top of the list of qualifications. Based on my conversation with executive recruiters, this is happening now but it wasn't before. It wasn't that boards didn't want ethical management, they just never insisted upon it. Companies and search firms must check out the potential CEO's ethics. Instead of just referencing business contacts, they should reference community leaders and even suppliers.

An ethical company begins with an ethical CEO. The CEO determines the tone of a company. If he or she isn't ethical, then somewhere, some time the company will most likely not be ethical.

On my first day at Russell in 1998, we discussed the operating principles that we expected everyone to live by. Fortunately, I had joined a company with strong values. I want to share these values with you.

Values from Russell Management Principles

1. It is essential to deal with honesty and integrity toward all: the company, shareholders, communities, customers, vendors, and each other.
2. Diversity is an important part of our culture and should be encouraged and nurtured at every opportunity. Diversity is not just race or gender but accepting everyone and considering their ideas regardless of their background.
3. Involvement in the community is an important Operating Principle. We should personally get involved in our communities to make them even better places to live and work.
4. We must treat people with respect and empower all employees. When difficult decisions have to be made to remain competitive, we should do everything possible to respect the employees who will be affected.

Our goal is to make these values a way of life at Russell. When we hire or promote people, these values are a must. We turn down many results-oriented executives with excellent track records to choose people who have a shared vision. If we make a hiring mistake, we try to correct it as rapidly as possible. Everything starts with values and ethics.

Having values does not mean that you can avoid making difficult decisions. We have all, unfortunately, watched a number of companies go out of business or into bankruptcy because the leaders couldn't make the tough and necessary changes to be competitive. All going down with the ship together is not the solution.

When we implemented our major restructuring program in order to be competitive, we had to downsize our U.S. organization from over 16,000 employees to less than 6,000 employees in a period of a little over three years. It wasn't something we wanted to do, and it was a very difficult decision to make.But it was a critical decision if we were to save the jobs of the 6,000 U.S. employees who were left. But as we did it, it was important for us to treat the people who were leaving the company fairly and with respect. It wasn't their fault that the global competitive situation had changed.

We established a program to help with the transition to their new careers. Not only did we pay attractive severance packages and extend medical benefits, but we provided training in their plants on how to get jobs and funds for further education. We had a moving allowance if someone wanted to relocate. We made transitional donations to charities in the communities we were leaving and even donated several plants to communities in order to help secure new employers.

As a result of all those efforts, most of our former employees obtained good jobs and twenty percent of them went for further education. Because we treated employees' leaving with respect, they knew we appreciated what they had done for the company . . . and the remaining employees felt better too.

In order to survive, many of those jobs eliminated were moved to Mexico or Central America. In setting up our operations there, we established the strongest operating principles to protect our employees and the environment. Not only do we extensively train employees, as many of them have never worked in structured jobs before, we provide attractive compensation, medical benefits, and importantly, a chance to better their lives. They now have the opportunity to own homes, many for the first time—to get further education for themselves and their children—to receive adequate medical care. The jobs created really do change people's lives.

We also strongly encourage all our operations and employees to get involved in the communities where they work and live, whether it is in Alabama, Atlanta, or Honduras. Nothing is more rewarding than seeing the impact on an orphanage in Honduras or a school in a country where people have very little, when you provide even the smallest amount of support.

Russell has gone through difficult times as we restructured but, fortunately, we are now anticipating sales and earnings growth this year despite the challenging environment. But even with the difficult times, among our first hires were a

Director of Diversity and a Vice President of Community Relations reporting directly to me. We wanted to ensure that our values were not only maintained but constantly reinforced. It is easy to have values in the good times, but true values are determined in the difficult times. For example, we consistently see a return on investment from our support of the communities where we have operations, especially when we did not reduce contributions even when our profits declined.

The same emphasis was put on diversity. Diversity must be a way of life for everyone. It can't be a short-term initiative. The CEO must walk the talk, as action speaks louder than words. When I joined Russell, I attended the Martin Luther King Day celebration in Alexander City, Alabama, where our headquarters and 5,000 employees were located. At that time, Russell did not give Martin Luther King Day as a holiday but we did give nine holidays, which was the upper range of companies in our industry. We couldn't afford to give an extra holiday as we were under tremendous competitive pressure. I proposed changing one of the other holidays to MLK Day, but this decision was not popular. MLK Day was viewed as a black holiday, not the celebration of freedom and rights for everyone that we know it truly is.

We made the decision that MLK Day was going to be a holiday. This was not a universally accepted decision but, again, leadership is about doing the right thing, not the popular thing. By the way, MLK Day in Alexander City is becoming much more of a community celebration rather than just a black holiday. Today there is also a community diversity task force that brings people together from many different backgrounds and last week they had over 500 people participate in their first Unity Walk through downtown.

For us, diversity is important because we know we can't be successful unless we respect and involve all our employees throughout our operations. Diversity is inclusion rather than exclusion, whether of different race, gender, religion, or just ideas. Today we have made great progress in building on our values and diversity, but we also know we have a long way to go. We can't mistake excellent progress for excellence. We have Latin American and African American Heritage Groups. And, we are in the process of training 100 percent of our U.S.-based employees in diversity. Our own employees have volunteered their time as facilitators to conduct these training programs on a 24/7 basis because we run the plants around the clock. These volunteers understand our diversity efforts are part of everyone's job. At times, I look at our company and say we have a long way to go, but then I get reminded of all we have accomplished.

Now, how does this relate to Restoring Corporate Trust? With the right corporate values, trust is never an issue in the first place. There never should be a question of what you should do because your ethics determine your response. With ethics, making the right decisions is easy; however, the decisions themselves may be very painful. If you would not be proud to see what you are doing publicized, you probably shouldn't be doing it.

When I was teaching at Wake Forest University, one of the sessions I taught was called, "Why do people do unethical things?"

First, unfortunately there are a small percentage of people who are dishonest. This group must be held accountable for their actions.

There is a slightly larger group that will be dishonest when they see a chance. Strong laws and monitoring can help control this group. Our new laws are directed at them.

But there is a larger group. People who will go with the flow—because everyone is doing it. They can convince themselves it isn't wrong ... it's just the way the game is played or how things are done.

In the 1980s we had the Wall Street insider trading scandal. A number of people were arrested. Many people seemed to have forgotten about that scandal and in the last few years, some people pushed the envelope doing unethical and even illegal things.

Many people did not see this as wrong, just like we don't see it as wrong when many of us choose to break the law every day. For instance, there are probably many people in this room today who choose to break the law because everyone is doing it. I am talking about speeding. But we say to ourselves that 70 or 75 miles per hour is the real speed limit, everyone does it. In fact, it would be dangerous not to speed, etc. It is socially accepted to speed—we perceive nothing wrong with it up to a point. I am not for or against speeding but it is an example of how people convince themselves that they are not doing the wrong thing, even when breaking a law. Strong ethical leadership is needed to determine the acceptable behavior within an organization.

Of course, Wall Street has even been known to encourage financial people to be creative and innovative. We want creative ability in a lot of areas, but not financial reporting. I would like to comment on the recent legislation called the Sarbanes-Oxley Act and the New York Stock Exchange Governances. For most companies, the key governance issues are not a new way to conduct business. Codes of Business Conduct, internal audit departments, certifying results, independent boards and committees, prohibiting executive loans, executive sessions of the board, etc., are all appropriate requirements and in many companies, like Russell, they have been the standard practice. I, too, believe there has to be a balance of power between the board and the CEO. Truly independent boards and audit, compensation, and governance committees are necessary. I have been shocked at the compensation abuse in some companies. CEOs should be paid fairly and share in the rewards if long-term results are achieved, but Boards must take a stronger position to prevent abuse.

I know at Russell, our management team has fair base salaries based on independent evaluations. They operate in a culture of accountability and if we deliver the results, expect to receive bonuses. If we miss our results, we don't expect to receive them. Last year, due to the weak economy, operating problems, and 9/11, we did not achieve our goals—despite a lot of exceptional effort. Thus, based on our results, many of us received no bonus. We had a compensation system with integrity.

One other important governance step is to ensure that all board members are there because they add value. They should bring knowledge and expertise. There is no room for someone on the board just because they are a friend of someone. On the other hand, we can't let legislation, publicity, and the threat of lawsuits drive away capable board members. Today, for example, it is extremely difficult for someone to be on an audit committee even if they are willing to accept the workload. If our company buys anything from a company, then a person from that company may not be able to be on the audit committee. There can be no direct or indirect benefit received. We need to have a reasonable level imposed. It is very difficult to find major corporations that have absolutely zero business with another one.

We now also have four separate financial required certifications, one by Congress, one by the SEC, one by the New York Stock Exchange, and one for the accounting firm. There has to be a way to simplify the process.

While the laws and regulations aren't perfect and the publicity has been damaging, I still believe companies can restore public confidence—and we must restore that trust. The first and foremost way, as we discussed, is hire a CEO and management team with ethics. Nothing else is needed if you accomplish this, because the CEO will establish a culture of ethics.

Second, Wall Street, shareholders, and boards of directors must encourage management to do the right things for the long run. This includes ethically building long-term relationships with all constituents, whether employees, communities, shareholders, customers, or suppliers.

Third, we must ensure a strong board of independent directors. But the board should not interfere in normal operating decisions.

Fourth, we need to publicize the many good things most companies are doing. Many outstanding, highly ethical companies have not received appropriate publicity. Too much is said about the unethical companies, yet the vast majority of public companies are highly ethical and doing the right things. I was very pleased to see this week's *Business Week* cover—entitled "The Good CEO. Yes, there are plenty of them."

Finally, we must remember that we have the greatest economic system and that it has created one of the highest living standards in the world. Let's make the necessary improvements, but don't throw the "baby out with the bath water."

CHAPTER FOUR

Ethical Governance and the Future of Free Enterprise

Steve Odland
Chairman and CEO, Office Depot Inc.
August 1, 2006

> I believe that the corporate model is changing as a result of all the recent reforms. Some of it is good, but we have to be careful about the unintended consequences of further change.

It's a pleasure to be here this afternoon to share my perspective on values, ethics, and corporate governance. Today, I'll speak to you both from the vantage point as CEO of Office Depot and also as Chairman of the Corporate Governance Task Force at the Business Roundtable.

In the past few years, we have suffered through a traumatic period of corporate and financial scandals in our country. These indignities really shook the trust and confidence of Americans who rely on business for jobs, for their savings, and for their retirement security. Public outrage followed these scandals—and rightly so. There were sensational disclosures of misdeeds. Federal and state officials reacted in turn by imposing new regulations on corporations in addition to all the regulations that we faced before that. These activities got the attention of government officials, of course, but also of those of us in the board rooms of companies around the country.

There are about 15,000 listed public companies in this country—and it's important to note that the vast majority of us who work in those companies try to do the right thing every single day and are good, decent people. We had a situation where there were a handful of people who did the wrong thing. Unfortunately, those bad apples tarnished the whole barrel. So, it's very important for us to speak up as business leaders and talk about corporate ethics—not only with our people, but also with people who are unfamiliar with corporations so that they understand the focus that we have and how important we think it is.

Responsible business people were embarrassed by these scandals. But we can't let the misdeeds of a few unscrupulous people undermine the public's trust in our economy. After all, when you think about our free market system and everything we know about it, it really has trust at its core. When you trade a stock, how do you know where it goes? If you think about the paper money that we carry in our wallet, who says it's worth what's printed on it? It's because we trust that there is value in our system. It's because we trust that when we press the "send" button on our computer, that money is actually flowing. So, all this is based on a foundation of trust.

We are living in a country that has the greatest amount of freedom in human history. We are part of the greatest superpower ever. Where does that come from? It came from the private sector building one of the greatest economies known to mankind. So, if you think about corporate scandals and corporate governance, it's not just a "nice to do" thing. It is an important "must do" in order to instill confidence and trust in our economy and thereby reinforce everything that we stand for in the country.

Let me just take a few minutes to describe some of the changes that corporate leaders have been making on their own. First of all, as a member of Business Roundtable, I'm very proud that we took the initiative to strengthen our corporate governance guidelines. We spelled out the rights and responsibilities among the various corporate participants, including management, boards of directors, and shareholders. The Roundtable's members are a group of 164 Chief Executive Officers of the largest companies in the nation. We have a combined workforce of over ten million people and $4.5 trillion in sales. That $4.5 trillion would be the third largest economy in the world after the United States and Japan. So, this is an important group of people who said, "We're going to stand up and we're going to speak out about corporate governance."

The Roundtable is committed to advocating public policies that ensure vigorous economic growth, a dynamic global economy, and the well-trained and productive U.S. workforce that is essential for our future competitiveness. We also believe that the basic interests of business closely parallel those of the American people as consumers, as employees, and as shareholders.

I've always had a strong personal interest in corporate governance. It's interesting to me to see how corporations work. When I became a CEO, my first question to the board was what are our guidelines, who is going to do what, how are we going to divide the duties, and what are our roles and accountabilities? Until a few years ago we didn't have anything called corporate governance guidelines. When I first started talking about corporate governance, people looked at me. They didn't know what that meant.

Think of how far we've come in just a very few years, when now corporate governance is debated in the classroom and at the kitchen table and our children pretty much know what we're talking about.

I was happy to chair the Corporate Governance Task Force of the Business Roundtable because of my interest. The Roundtable's involvement in reform goes back a quarter of a century and it culminated in the issuance of our best practices publication in 2002 entitled *Principles of Corporate Governance*. By the way, you can access anything that I refer to today on the BRT's Website, www.brt.org.

When we printed this—and I had a hand in drafting that pamphlet—it was at the very beginning of the corporate scandals; the height was later, unfortunately. The Roundtable recommended some things that were really radical at the time—and you'll probably laugh because they don't seem so radical today.

First of all, we said that the majority of corporate boards of directors must be independent, both in appearance and reality—those are two different things—and that the board should choose the CEO and require that the corporation act in a competent and ethical way. I know you will say to me, "Well of course that's what corporate governance guidelines should say," but there weren't corporate governance guidelines and nobody was saying that that's what they should say as recently as 2002.

Second, we said senior management must produce shareholder value. Again, that's why we're all there, but at the same time that wasn't viewed in the same sentence as corporate ethics. We said they weren't mutually exclusive. You can never put personal interest ahead of the customers, employees, and shareholders.

Third, directors and senior managers must produce financial statements and timely disclosures that fairly present to investors the financial condition and results of the corporation.

Fourth, directors and their audit committees are responsible for hiring the independent auditor to approve financial statements prepared by the management team, and to ensure the independence of that outside auditor.

Fifth, the auditor must be independent in fact, apply the highest standards to its work, and report any concerns to the audit committee and board. Finally, the corporation must deal with employees in a fair and ethical manner.

There's nothing revolutionary in there. But those recommendations probably sound familiar today because so many of them were adopted by Congress shortly after our publication when it passed the landmark Public Company Accounting Reform and Investor Protection Act. Nobody can remember that, so we call it the Sarbanes-Oxley Act. It was a moment of rare bipartisan action in response to the breakdown in the corporate checks and balances that cost investors hundreds of billions of dollars in losses. The Roundtable and I strongly supported the Sarbanes-Oxley Act. It was difficult, but it was necessary if you think about where we were. Think about the risk of what could have happened if we had lost public trust in the economy and in business.

We followed up those recommendations a year later by spelling out the *Principles of Executive Compensation*. What we were trying to do was to lay out some sensible ways to link executive pay with performance. We spelled out the role of the compensation committee in actually understanding what they were approving in levels of executive pay. That seems like a stunningly obvious recommendation, but if you think through the scandals and concerns that have come to light in the past few years, a lot of them were around boards and compensation committees who were actually not understanding what they were approving.

You're always looking through the windshield of a car as you're driving. You're thinking about the things you put in place because these are our intended consequences—this is what we're trying to drive in terms of corporate expectations and so forth. The problem is we don't think about unintended consequences. We don't think about all the "what ifs" that could happen later. If you see outrageous packages go to failed CEOs, you say, "How could that happen?" It's because nobody goes into a situation planning for failure. Therefore, you have unintended consequences.

Other recommendations from the Business Roundtable included that pay must be linked to performance and that only independent directors should be on the compensation committee. That's required by law today, but it wasn't at the time that we recommended it. We also recommended that outside experts be used. This is controversial today because everybody says that's why salaries are going up. But at the same time, not everybody on a compensation committee is a compensation expert. So, we recommend that people use experts in order to put together appropriate packages.

We were pleased with the SEC's move to require more and better disclosure of executive pay, including stock option backdating. Again, this is bitter medicine in some ways, but the change in proxy reporting is probably a good thing. If you think about it, it's better to disclose and be transparent about what's going on in the company than to surprise people later.

Beyond these improved standards, the Business Roundtable also strongly supported regulatory reforms that made constructive business practices the law of the land. We've supported the changes to the listing standards for New York Stock Exchange and NASDAQ listed public corporations. These significantly strengthened financial and governance standards.

Four years after the passage of the Sarbanes-Oxley Act, we can say that the reforms are taking hold. Many Roundtable member corporations have already adopted them in advance of regulations, and some have gone beyond required standards.

Let me be very specific. We do a survey every year of corporate governance practices among our member firms. Again, it's only 164 companies, but $4.5 trillion in sales; and these companies account for one-third of the total market cap of the entire country, on all the stock exchanges put together. So it's an important survey.

We found that in the last year, 60 percent of our companies have improved or increased the emphasis on the pay-per-performance element of their senior executive compensation. More than 90 percent of companies today have an independent chairman, lead director or presiding director. That's up from 70 percent just a couple of years ago. It's a big, big change in corporate governance. Seventy percent of companies reported that independent directors met in executive session at every board meeting. Ninety-plus percent have established procedures for shareholder communications directly with the board. The survey also shows that the costs of Sarbanes-Oxley compliance appear to be leveling off. Over half of our companies now say that they are expecting compliance costs to go down in the coming year. Only 6 percent expect it to go up. So it looks like the cost of

Sarbanes-Oxley implementation has been borne and should now be coming down in the next few years. The cost is about $10 million a year on an average for our member companies going forward.

In addition to wide acceptance of these reforms among public companies, many private companies—and I know that there are a number in the room—are adopting the corporate governance guidelines, listing standards, and so forth. This is partially because they want the ability to go public, partially because they want the ease of sale to other public companies, and partially that they just want to do the right thing—or what they see as being the most advanced way to run their company. In short, corporate leaders are responding to both the letter and the spirit of the new laws and regulations that have been issued in the past few years.

Or to put it another way, "so far so good." But the real question is, where do we go from here? I'd like to answer that question first by talking about some concerns about the system and then discussing some of our principles and values. Concerns first: We have now lived through the last five years where we have seen more change in corporate governance and more change in the way we approach our shareholders and employees than we have in probably the previous thirty to forty years. That's a lot of change for corporate America to absorb.

Unfortunately, for some people the changes and the dramatic improvement in corporate governance have only spelled an appetite for more change, and the problem is that at some point you've got to stop changing; you've got to start letting things settle out. What we are worried about is that the new changes may fall victim to unintended consequences; that in addition to trying to fix what's wrong, we could break what's right. That's a concern. The famous sociologist Robert Merton wrote in the 1930s about what he called "unanticipated consequences," and that's what we need to avoid. We can't strive so hard to rid ourselves of every possible thing that could go wrong that we just put a collar on all our economic growth.

Imagine what would happen to this country if all innovation was squeezed out of these companies. Now you may say, "What does corporate governance have to do with innovation? Those are two different things." But the fact of the matter is that what we do every single day is to manage risk. We manage risk by saying what we're going to bet on, what we're going to try to do differently. We've got to do things differently in our companies in order to grow and change and produce more shareholder value. My favorite quote is—and the people from Office Depot will probably be able to recite this in their sleep—that "the definition of insanity is doing the same thing over and over again and expecting different results." The point is that you can't keep doing the same things and expect results to be different.

People usually use the quote when things are going wrong. It's when things are going right that they really ought to be nervous. That's when doing things over and over again still does not make sense. So change generally is good, but we have to avoid constant change in our corporate governance structure so that we do not, in fact, choke off innovation.

One of the keys to business success, especially in our global marketplace, is risk-taking. We've got to be careful not to criminalize honest mistakes. Who here has never made a mistake? None of us. That's what I worry about at night. Talking to many of you around the room, I'm sure you do as well. We're just trying to do the right thing every single day, but we're human beings and we're going to make mistakes. But if you say that every mistake is going to be a criminal offense, where are we going to be?

Recently a bill was introduced in Congress that would make it a felony for any CEO to sell any product that had any defect. At Office Depot we sell 8,500 items; we don't manufacture them. There is probably a 99 percent rate of compliance with these products, but no manufacturer can be perfect every time. But they want to criminalize these mistakes.

Now I don't think this bill is going to go through, because I think that some people up there have the common sense to know that we cannot criminalize normal mistakes. Otherwise we all might as well retire and do something else.

A philosopher said that the risk of a wrong decision is preferable to the terror of indecision. That's one of the things that we have to think about as we go forward.

There are other dangers, too. Most of you are probably long-term investors, but the average holding period for investors now is down to nine and a half months on the New York Stock Exchange. Today, hedge funds account for over 50 percent of the volume on the stock exchanges. They're flipping the stocks every couple of months. They used to be called shareholders; they're traders today. I think the vast majority of investors really are focused on long-term enhanced shareholder value, but there are groups out there with different agendas. This is another concern of ours. We have groups pushing social agendas—whether it's pension reform, or environment, or health care. These are all appropriate things for groups to be working on, but these are people who are trying to earn a place at the board table.

I believe that in the coming years, these groups probably will try to use boards of directors to make changes in society that they cannot achieve through federal or state legislation. In effect, they are trying to create a new corporate model, one in which the corporation turns into a virtual New England town meeting. This is not all bad, but it's not all good. You see the shareholder access efforts, the majority vote efforts, and so forth of these various interest groups trying to gain access to the boardrooms. Then you see various proposals coming through to require every decision in the board room to be unanimous or to allow access to the board room. You can start to see a progression here that's disconcerting, particularly when there are other agendas being worked by these people.

The concern is that these agendas are unrelated to long-term performance of companies. So the question I think we have to ask is, what is the impact on the fundamental mission of the corporation—which is to generate shareholder value over the long term, to fuel productivity, to create jobs, and to strengthen the economy.

I believe that the corporate model is changing as a result of all the recent reforms. Some of it is good, but we have to be careful about the unintended consequences of further change. The challenge for all of us as institutional investors, corporate leaders, and community leaders is to make sure that we have a corporate model that can maintain public trust while creating economic growth, jobs, and value for investors. John Jacques Rousseau said, "Good laws lead to the making of better ones, bad ones bring about worse." We have to be careful. History is going to judge Sarbanes-Oxley by what comes next.

Let me talk a little bit about principles.

Former Deputy Attorney General and now Law Professor Larry Thompson noted that every fresh business scandal brings calls for new regulations to prevent such a scandal from ever happening again. "Regulations expand with each ensuing scandal to encompass every possible abuse—except the next one," he stated. That's not to say, of course, that we should abandon regulations. But we need to understand that real, lasting change can only come from improving corporate cultures, and by a genuine commitment to ethical behavior. That involves moving beyond rules-based corporate behavior to values-based behavior. We've got to have people in organizations doing the right thing, even when the rules don't precisely cover it or when they don't think that anyone's watching.

To that end, the Business Roundtable established the Institute for Corporate Ethics at the Darden School at the University of Virginia in partnership with leading business schools around the country in order to help strengthen the links between ethics and business practices. The Institute conducts research and seminars in business ethics, is creating a cutting-edge business ethics curriculum, leads executive seminars on business ethics, and develops best practices in corporate ethics. I know that some of you in the room and the universities are involved with that and I think it's really terrific.

At our request, the Institute staff polled the Roundtable CEOs about the ethical questions they face and their priorities. You know we don't really face the specter of theft or fraud every single day; that rarely happens and hopefully none of us has to deal with that. The ethical things that we deal with every day are all the shades of gray: should you outsource jobs, jobs vs. pricing, where do you put manufacturing, how do you keep your cost structure in line in order to take care of your customers while at the same time making sure you have high-paying jobs? These are the kinds of ethical questions that we deal with every single day.

In the poll, we found that establishing a framework of how to approach decision-making that integrates ethics is a top priority. We also found that ethics and strength in corporate governance are absolutely required for long-term business success.

There's been a lot of debate about whether corporate governance leads us to better corporate performance. A lot of people say, "No, there's no direct link," and maybe there isn't. But over the long term we see the companies that are focused and doing the right thing are those companies that do well.

For example, people still mention the Johnson & Johnson recall of Extra Strength Tylenol in 1982 as a model for ethical behavior. When eight people died from the deliberate poisoning of capsules, the company responded immediately. I'm not even sure if they had a meeting; they just acted and pulled Tylenol off the shelves of every store in this country. That move cost them over half a billion dollars in profits. It was a masterful public relations move, but it was really more than that. I think it was a reflection of their corporate values. From the CEO on down, Johnson & Johnson shared the belief that it was their duty to protect the health of their customers before thinking about their shareholders. Sometimes you have to make those trade-offs.

I remember my constituencies every morning because it's my title—CEO: Customers, Employees, and Owners. Some people add community and other constituencies, but I call those customers. Customers, Employees, and Owners—you have to balance those three constituencies. I think that in this example, Johnson & Johnson struck the right balance. They demonstrated that they were serious about upholding their values and reassuring the public that Tylenol was safe. So when they reintroduced the product about six weeks later with tamper-proof packaging—which I think was the first tamper-proof packaging in this country—they quickly regained sales leadership. They lost a lot of money, but at the same time they preserved the franchise and today it is still the leader. I think they set a reassuring standard of ethical conduct, especially when contrasted with companies that take half measures and try to shift blame when they meet similar challenges. Likewise, business leaders and investors more than ever believe that companies with the best governance are the best-performing companies. There's a recent study by Professor J.D. Margolis of Harvard, who looked at forty-two studies of the subject and found a strong correlation among corporate social responsibility, high ethical standards, and corporate financial success.

Integrating ethical values in everyday decision-making doesn't happen by accident. Instead, it requires certain conditions. First of all, people need to know what we stand for as CEOs, or as leaders of any organization. That involves a clear statement of ethical principles. Second, employees and officers need to be able to push back. Where you have fear in the company that it's not OK to say, "Wait a minute; I'm not sure that I agree," then you have a situation that's ripe for unethical behavior. You've got to be able to report wrongdoing, oppose improvements without any fear of retribution. Everybody has a hotline now because you're supposed to have one, but at the same time people are afraid in many cases—and you've got to make sure that the fear is gone. So in addition to the practices, you have to make sure that the values system is there.

Third, there needs to be access to management for everyone from customers to shareholders. Fourth, the organization needs to be transparent and open; and fifth, everyone in the corporation needs to understand how we're supposed to treat each other. You learned about these principles in kindergarten, right? They are not rocket science, but that's what our people are saying.

At Office Depot, we work hard to make sure that we have the highest level of ethical standards. We're not perfect, but we do our best. For example—and I'm sure you all have done similar things—we have a confidential ethics hotline that's staffed by an independent third party, not company staff, in order to make it comfortable for people to call.

We have an executive compensation system that attempts to practice what we preach. Our compensation for executives is made up of base, bonus, and then equity, and the vast majority of our compensation is at risk. The full payoff of our compensation comes when we meet multiple targets set by an independent compensation committee. It truly is performance-based; if we don't succeed, we don't get the reward. Now, if we get the rewards, it is pay-per-performance because the shareholders will win first.

We also stress ethics training at Office Depot. Besides requiring everybody to sign an annual statement affirming compliance with our code, we also require everyone to do online training—and there's a test. I did this a couple of weeks ago; I have to do it every year just like anybody at Office Depot. It's a white-knuckle process; can you imagine if I got something wrong on that test? It was stressful, but I got through it. The system provides information about our code of ethics, and then quizzes people on how to apply it to numerous situations. It really makes people think and not just memorize.

We try to make sure that people understand our code of ethics, but more importantly we take a values-based approach for our company. I'm really proud of our values, because every word was articulated by our officer team.

Recently our board of directors amended our corporate governance bylaws with the provision that any director who fails to receive a majority vote will resign from the board and they will deal with their resignation. I think this latest initiative reinforces our commitment to listen to our shareholders and be responsive to their concerns.

Most of us are trying to put the right systems and processes in place, but strong corporate governance and ethical standards are not simply matters of personal and public morality. They are also essential for long-term success. The indiscretions that have happened were thought to be shortcuts to success, but in fact what they have done is distorted and ultimately betrayed our free market system.

Unethical behavior and even outright corruption discourage hard work on the part of associates, degrade our productivity and our competitiveness, cheapen our daily lives, and weaken the bonds of trust—and really, who wants to live in a society like that?

Why are we here? Why do we live in this country? Partially because we were born here, but partially because we choose to stay. We choose to stay because we think it's the greatest place in the world. That is driven by a foundation of ethics—corporate ethics, personal ethics, and government ethics. A corporation and a society based on strong governance principles and high ethical standards are in the best position to face the unexpected challenges. Clearly we have a lot of those in our country today. We are going to have challenges from now until the time that we leave here; that's just the way it's going to be. But you've always got to have the roots and a foundation of ethical principles to fall back on. If we do that, I think our country will overcome any challenge and will flourish. As long as we can keep that idea central, we can continue to look forward to a twenty-first century that has the highest level of prosperity and human progress ever in history.

CHAPTER FIVE

What Can the World's Religions Tell Us about Ethics in Business?

Edward Zinbarg
Retired Chief Investment Officer, Chief Administrative Officer, and Chief Financial Officer, The Prudential Life Insurance Company
November 14, 2002

> The cultural underpinnings of billions—yes billions—of people in the world are religious. Therefore, it would be seem prudent to know something about those religious influences even if one is not personally religious.

The Bible says that Moses kept detailed financial records of donations given by the Israelites to build the tabernacle in the desert. Significantly, in the context of recent business scandals in America, the classic rabbinic commentaries on the text suggest that Moses also appointed independent auditors to make sure that no one could accuse him of keeping any of the donations for himself.

The Rabbis believed that even a man who spoke directly to God felt an obligation to keep accurate financial records and have them independently audited. Clearly, concerns about dishonest accounting and dishonest executives are by no means unique to modern times. They have always been with us and surely will continue to be with us—no matter what new government regulations are put in place. For one of the constants of human nature is its dual nature.

All of us act nobly at some times and downright rotten at other times. The same business executive can sometimes be kind and compassionate to his associates, and at other times be quite ruthless. A religious person can be tolerant in some circumstances, yet at other times behave as if only he or she had the keys to the Kingdom.

As a trained economist and businessman, I am a strong believer in the social progress that comes with a vigorously competitive marketplace that rewards efficiency and effectiveness. But there must be boundaries between competing vigorously and being a scoundrel. Where those boundaries lie is the big question. It's a question I have probed by studying what the great religious traditions of the world have had to say about the subject.

Why bring religion into the picture? What is the relevance of religious teachings to a commercial world that was never envisioned in religious scriptures?

To my mind, the question of relevance may be more appropriate for issues in, say, biomedical ethics than for business ethics. Biomedicine is dealing with technologies that were inconceivable in the ancient world; yet, it is common for hospitals to have religious figures on their ethics panels.

That being the case, I would argue that it is even more appropriate to bring religious perspectives into issues of business ethics. For while modern biotechnology was inconceivable to the ancients, people have been engaged in trade for at least 5,000 years; and most of the basic ethical issues of today's marketplace were quite familiar to ancient sages, even if the specific ways the issues arise are somewhat different. As I noted, even Moses was concerned that he not be accused of cooking the books.

You also may ask why a person of one faith, in my case Jewish, should be interested in what people of other faiths think about business ethics. Indeed, you may ask whether people with no religious affiliation at all should be interested in religious attitudes toward business ethics.

One reason they should, is that more and more businesses operate in a global marketplace. So they have to deal with people of many different cultures. And the fact is that the cultural underpinnings of billions—yes billions—of people in the world are religious. Therefore, it would be seem prudent to know something about those religious influences even if one is not personally religious.

And if you *do* identify with some religious tradition, it is usually the case that as you gain insights into other traditions, you broaden and deepen your understanding of your own.

A final reason why anyone, religious or not, should be interested in the subject is simply that the great religious thinkers of history were very smart people. The Buddha, Moses, Jesus, Muhammad, and other such religious figures had great insights into life and the human psyche. You don't have to accept the theological basis of their ideas to get value from their keen ethical insights.

I'd like, now, to do two things. First, give you a quick overview of the similarities and differences in the business ethics of the six major religious traditions I've studied—Jewish, Christian, Muslim, Hindu, Buddhist, and Confucian. Second, I want to focus on a particular aspect of the subject, ethics in the workplace.

There are certainly different theological starting points in the different traditions. The religious ethics of the Western world, which is basically monotheistic, originate with scriptures that describe divine commands. Asian religious ethics, on the other hand, originate, by and large, with metaphysical philosophies about the nature of the universe and the meaning of life—somewhat like the Wisdom Literature within the Bible, such as Psalms, Proverbs, Job, Ecclesiastes.

In addition to different starting points, there are differences of ethical emphasis. For example, I would argue that Jewish tradition has tended to be more pragmatic than Christian tradition. And within Christianity, Catholic ethical thought has tended to be more pragmatic than Protestant ideas.

Moreover, while all religions value compassion, it is probably a more pronounced value in Buddhism than in other traditions. And in the *Hindu* view of life, the importance of humility and patience sometimes seems to permit ethical behavior that people with other backgrounds would be less patient with—such as the caste system.

Speaking of caste distinctions, there is a regrettable similarity in all six religious traditions. They all have a history of negative attitudes toward the roles and rights of women, although some have been attempting to change these attitudes.

Despite their theological differences and some of their different emphases, all six of these major religious traditions reach remarkably similar conclusions about behavior in the marketplace. Let me briefly outline them.

1. They all accept a seller's need to put his best foot forward, but denounce deliberate deceit in the process of making the sale.
2. They all recognize the hard realities of the workplace, but they teach that human beings should not be treated as if they were mere commodities.
3. They caution against selling harmful products, price gouging essential goods, and damaging the natural environment in the process of producing goods and services.
4. They denounce bribery and call on professional people to be worthy of the special trust that is placed in them.
5. They ask lenders to be willing to suspend their legal rights in order to assist borrowers in distress.

These similarities are remarkable and, I think, provide a good basis for interfaith dialogue on specific ways to apply these general principles to specific cases. On that score, I'd like, now, to consider some religious attitudes toward ethics in the workplace.

All religious traditions assert that employment confers dignity on people and, hence, is an important component of a good and meaningful life. However, my research suggests that religious communities have not had a uniform view of the basic relationship between employers and employees. To describe the differences, I will focus on Jewish and Christian views. First, let's take a look at the Jewish approach.

In general, Jewish economic ethics begins with recognition that there are two social values that are good in themselves, but often are in conflict. Therefore, they need to be balanced. One value is *efficiency*, whose benefit is that it enhances the material well being of society. The other value is *equity*, which reflects God's demand for justice and harmony among human beings.

To illustrate how this need for balance plays out in the workplace, Jewish ethics begins with an assumption that, more often than not, workers can find employment elsewhere if they don't like a particular employer's offer; and employers can usually find other workers to replace them. In general, therefore, workers and employers are seen in Jewish tradition as having no special obligations to each other beyond their employment agreement. This is believed to foster maximum efficiency. I refer to it in my book as a "contractual" approach to the employer-employee relationship.

To be sure, Jewish tradition recognizes that employers usually have more staying power than their workers. Therefore, while the contract they enter into may be *legally* controlling, employers are urged to interpret the contract with generosity, in the interest of equity. Moreover, Jewish tradition does not simply rely on an employer's generosity to achieve equity. It has strongly supported labor unions and collective bargaining to overcome the power imbalance. But here, too, the focus is on the contract that the two sides enter into.

Christian understandings of the employment relationship seem to me somewhat different from the Jewish perspective.

Saint Paul's letters to the fledgling Christian communities of his day contain a great deal of practical advice in addition to their theological insights. As I read his letters, two key principles seem to emerge regarding the workplace. The first emphasizes individual effort and individual responsibility. Honest work is ennobling, Paul asserts, and laziness should not be tolerated. But the second Pauline principle, I think, is that individual effort and responsibility are meaningful only within a mutually supportive relationship between employers and employees.

Paul's call for reciprocity in employment relationships has counterparts, I believe, in the Gospels. Consider, for example, the parable of the Laborers in the Vineyard (Matthew, Chapter 20). In this story, an employer hires some day laborers at the going rate. He later hires others to work less than a day, without stipulating the wage but indicating that he will pay what is fair.

At the end of the day, he pays *all* the laborers the full day's rate, including those who worked less than a day. When the full-day workers complain, the employer points out that the full-day workers got exactly what they expected, and they should not be envious that the part-timers got more than they probably expected.

On a theological level, this story may be seen as a parable about God's merciful nature. Although some Christians (indeed, some Jews as well) think that God dispenses His grace in a carefully calculated, quid-pro-quo fashion, most believers think of God's mercy as limitless.

From the perspective of workplace ethics, I think that the message of this Gospel story is similar. Employers and employees, the story suggests, should think of themselves as part of a family that willingly shares its fortunes and misfortunes. I refer to this in my book as a "covenantal" approach to the relationship. As in a marriage, or in the biblical covenant between God and Israel, both of which do have contractual aspects, the mutual obligations of the parties go far beyond the contract. That, I think, is the New Testament's desire for relationships between employers and employees.

Roman Catholic papal encyclicals carry forward this New Testament theme of reciprocity in the workplace. In 1991, for example, Pope John Paul II said in *Centesimus Annus*: "The Church acknowledges the legitimate role of profit as an indication that a business is functioning well. But profitability is not the only indicator of a firm's condition.... The purpose of a business firm ... is to be found in its very existence as a community of persons . . . at the service of the whole of society."

In using the term, "community of persons," I think the Pope was highlighting the idea that Christian ethics sees employer-employee relationships more in a *covenantal* than a *contractual* context. This viewpoint also shows up repeatedly in various Catholic "moral manuals," which are volumes that advise parish priests and laymen how to apply broad Catholic principles to specific situations.

While Protestant denominations rarely speak with a uniform voice, I believe that there is a fairly consistent theme in Protestant views on ethical issues. The theme has often been referred to as "Christian love," the idea being that "as Christ loved all the world, so shall you love each other."

I've taken a look at what the great figures in Protestant history have said about Christian love in the workplace. Some of their sermons have a very conservative tone, while some call for radical social change. I don't have the time, here, to discuss that long history. What I do want to refer to, however, are the views of some prominent modern businessmen who are lay leaders in various Protestant churches.

Typical of such businessmen is Max De Pree, who used to lead Herman Miller, Inc., a major office furniture company and a prominent lay leader in the Evangelical community. De Pree believed strongly that Christian love requires a covenantal rather than a contractual relationship between employers and employees. Indeed, he argued that in modern times, when competitive pressures have become more intense than ever, contractual relationships are more resistant to necessary change than covenantal relationships.

De Pree insisted that a covenantal view need not submerge the individuality so prized in American society. Just as people can be cooperative participants in a *family* without submerging their individuality, he said, so, too, can individuality shine in a covenantal business enterprise.

Nor, in his opinion, does a covenantal view mean that jobs are secure irrespective of an individual's performance or of the firm's profitability. Covenant does not mean there would be no corporate downsizing; but De Pree argued that the need for it would be reduced because covenantal firms would be more competitive.

My own view—perhaps because I am Jewish not Christian—is that the issue of downsizing poses a serious challenge to proponents of a covenantal view of the workplace. The analogy between workplace relationships and family relationships fails to recognize that a good parent cannot "dismiss a child" for poor performance—either the child's poor personal performance, or the family's poor financial performance.

Moreover, I think that the forces of global competition have further strained the analogy between workplace and family. Global business firms have workers abroad as well as domestically. So, not only are there different groups of domestic workers, whose interests may be different—for example, full-time workers versus part-time workers—but the interests of the foreign workers may be quite different from the domestic workers. Thus, even if a business manager tries to focus on "the common good," it may not be at all clear what the common good is.

These are the kinds of challenges that a contractual approach tries to overcome. The best way to avoid conflict, it asserts, is to agree to the rules of the game in advance and not depend too much on implied responsibilities, as you might in a family situation.

However, both the Jewish contractual and the Christian covenantal views of the workplace emphasize that workers are different from machines and raw materials. They stress that employers must treat workers with dignity and respect.

In conclusion, whatever your role is in either the workplace or in other parts of the marketplace, I urge you to consider that there has been an important missing element in most books, seminars, and other discussions of business ethics. The missing element is the wisdom of thousands of years of religious insight.

PART II

Ethical Concerns of Industry Sectors and Other Fields

The Ethical Crises in the Accounting and Auditing Profession

James E. Copeland, Jr.
Retired Chairman and CEO, Deloitte & Touche
September 20, 2005

> I believe we are at a high water mark for financial reporting, with almost everyone making an intense effort to report fairly and honestly. On the other hand, I believe it is unlikely that the Big Four firms will survive.

We are facing an ethical crisis in our society today that has been years in the making. The ethical consensus among our fellow citizens has been deteriorating for a long time, so the loss of an ethical consensus in our society should not have been a surprise.[1]

For example, about fifteen years ago, a small group of our Partners at Deloitte was asked by our CEO at the time to identify long-term threats to the viability of our firm and our profession. As part of that group, I suggested that the potential loss of consensus within our society around the prevailing set of ethical standards posed the greatest threat. I argued that this threat was particularly dangerous to our profession because auditors are highly dependent on honest representations by the management of our clients, and we also rely heavily on the ethical and competent performance of tens of thousands of our professionals every day. For these reasons, I suggested that a loss of integrity, competence, and ethics in our clients or our people would be devastating to our firm and our profession.

Unfortunately, we watched this exact scenario play out in the collapse of Enron, the demise of Andersen, and the series of scandals that has followed.

These ethical failures in the business community have taken a terrible toll. They have:

- destroyed some of the world's largest companies and hundreds of billions of dollars in shareholder value;
- put hundreds of thousands of people out of work with little or no warning or severance pay;
- shattered retirement plans and investments;

- undermined the trust we've placed in publicly reported financial information;
- eroded confidence in our capital markets;
- and ruined the good name and reputation of hundreds of thousands of people who spent their entire careers working in the capital markets with honesty and integrity.

And unfortunately the problem is even worse than this litany of horrors— because it is much more pervasive. It is important to recognize that our entire society—not just the business community—is facing an ethical breakdown of crisis proportions. Every sector of our society, from business to education to government to the press and to the church, is experiencing its own ethical failures.

And despite the wishful thinking of people in some other countries, this is not just an American phenomenon; it's a global pandemic.

As we sift through the financial and human wreckage in our society, searching for clues to what went wrong, the only common denominator seems to be unethical behavior and a lack of character and integrity.

Perhaps we should leave the causal factors to the historians and the behavioral scientists or our religious leaders. The more pressing question is how do we deal with this societal crisis? The challenge seems overwhelming. I believe that the only way we'll deal with this problem as a society is for each sector to come to grips with its own specific concerns. Hence, I'd like to focus today on the problems of the accounting and auditing profession, and encourage the academic community to become involved in the reconstruction of the accounting and auditing profession.

Engagement by the academic community is essential, because so much of the so-called "reform" of our society and our profession seems to be based on perception and popular notions rather than rigorous research and empirical evidence. We desperately need objective analytical capability to help us make sound decisions rather than "sound bite" decisions.

What are the scandal-related problems of the accounting and auditing profession? I would put the problems we face in three categories: (1) perception problems; (2) real problems, but not ethical in nature; and (3) genuine ethical problems. Let's talk about each of these categories.

PERCEPTION PROBLEMS

Probably the best example of perceived problems that seem to have little or no basis in fact is the whole scope of services/auditor independence issue. Critics focused principally on both the nature and amount of consulting and tax services provided by firms to their audit clients. The fact is that there is little anecdotal or empirical evidence that these services provided by audit firms to their clients result in reporting problems. In fact, much of the research shows that audit firms providing nonaudit services for audit clients had a neutral or positive impact on the quality of their audit work. The fallback position of our critics is always a question of the "appearance" or "perception" of independence. The rebuttal, of course, is that auditors are paid for audits by their audit clients—does that constitute less of an appearance problem?

Government auditors are arguably perfectly "independent," but government auditors and examiners have not, to my knowledge, produced more effective audits of entities with fewer problems in their financial statements. Certainly, the S&L (Savings & Loan) scandals were not avoided even though they were audited by both federal and state examiners. But with little or no empirical evidence to support the decision, we have now virtually dismantled the four most capable accounting and auditing firms in the world. This may, in fact, help cure the perception problem. Unfortunately, it creates the very real problem of reducing the competency of auditing firms by eliminating highly specialized capabilities necessary to audit sophisticated businesses. We are in danger of appearing independent by becoming incompetent. Perception does govern our actions, but reality determines the consequences.

Another common misperception is that the auditors were direct participants in frauds. Unfortunately, a number of corporate accounting professionals were involved directly in fraud; however, auditors seldom have been found to be guilty of sins other than incompetence. But that is not the public perception. For example, Senator Daschle said in New York on television, "Arthur Andersen drove Enron into the side of a mountain." Now Andersen may have performed an inadequate audit, but as far as I know they were not "piloting the plane" to continue the senator's metaphor. Because of the requirement for annual audits of publicly traded companies, a major auditing firm has been associated with virtually all the companies that suffered financial reporting scandals. In a few of these situations they did not do their jobs well. In rare instances, they did incompetent work, and we paid dearly for it. But actually participating in a fraud for personal benefit is something that almost never happens in the auditing profession.

While these and other perception problems are not real, they have resulted in the onerous and damaging "reforms" affecting our profession. There were professors who provided excellent research on some of these perception issues, and even though the evidence was largely ignored by the lawmakers and regulators in the political rush to "do something," their efforts were deeply appreciated by those in the auditing profession.

REAL PROBLEMS NOT INVOLVING ETHICS

In the second category of problems, the accounting and auditing profession has also had to face three issues that are real, but not ethical in nature. These problems might be described as three "gaps."

The first "gap" is "Generally Accepted Accounting Principles." The readers of financial statements are too often misled by what *The Economist* magazine referred to as the "brittle illusion of exactitude" of the current accounting model. The people in this room understand the "approximate" nature of financial reporting, but a gap exists between what financial statements represent and what many readers believe they represent. This "gap" appears to be growing as the FASB (Financial Accounting Standards Board) moves toward "fair value" accounting.

The second "gap" is the result of the rapidly increasing complexity of business activity and financial transactions, exacerbated by financial instruments designed to accomplish a specific business purpose and be accounted for in a specific way. Neither accountants nor auditors have been able to keep up with the complexity. Hence, a complexity—competency gap has been created that challenges our profession. FIN46 is just the latest manifestation of this "competency gap."

The third "gap" relates to auditors and represents the difference between the "reasonable assurance" offered by auditors and the "insurance" expected by many investors. For example, the general public and business press appears to believe auditors should detect collusive fraud at the time it happens. Auditors do not have criminal investigative tools—such as subpoenas, etc. And auditors do not know how to consistently detect sophisticated collusive fraud. This "expectation gap" is responsible for much of the loss of credibility of the auditing profession.

While these three "gaps" are not ethical issues, they are part of the problem of the overall impression that the public has of the auditing profession. Hopefully the academic community will play a role in helping to close or narrow these three "gaps."

GENUINE ETHICAL PROBLEMS

While some of the problems facing the accounting and auditing profession are a matter of perception and others are the consequences of the three "gaps" described above, the profession also faced a third category of problems—legitimate ethical problems.

Some corporate accountants became players in "making the numbers" even when operating results were clearly short of expectations. In a few instances they were even directly involved in fraudulent activities for personal gain. Auditors too often lacked the professional skepticism required in those circumstances and allowed too much to be swept under the rug of "materiality."

The auditing profession became involved in activities that represented clear conflicts of interest. These included some firms having investment banking relationships with their audit clients. Others had financial relationships with software vendors that were not always disclosed to consulting clients to whom they were recommending software. In some instances, firms entered into business relationships with their audit clients. While these inappropriate relationships were infrequent and limited, they gave regulators legitimate reasons to be suspicious and skeptical of the auditing profession.

Growth became too much of a concern for audit firms as competition grew increasingly fierce. This infected the compensation systems, and "rainmakers" sometimes became overvalued and overrewarded, creating a culture that did not sufficiently discourage unethical behavior.

Both corporate accountants and their auditors sometimes helped to shape transactions to "qualify" for a certain type of accounting treatment, even when the economic substance of the treatment would be more accurately reflected under a different accounting treatment. While these treatments might well be "in accordance with generally accepted accounting principles," they did not always "present fairly" the economic substance of the transaction. In those instances, accountants and auditors failed to live up to their responsibility to the investing public.

Finally, accountants and their auditors too often did not have sufficient courage and character to stand up to the intimidation of aggressive senior management. Pressured with threats of replacement or enticed by financial rewards, corporate accountants cooked up accounting schemes they knew to be inappropriate. When senior management threatened to change firms or ask for new partners, these questionable accounting treatments were sometimes rationalized and accepted by their outside auditors. Management of the auditing firms sometimes did not have adequate support structures in place to assure that these partners did the right thing even if it cost the firm an important client relationship.

Many of these ethical challenges and other problems were addressed by the Panel on Audit Effectiveness, created by the Public Oversight Board, at the request of Chairman Arthur Levitt and chaired by Shawn O'Malley, retired chairman of Price Waterhouse. The Executive Summary of the panel's report concluded with the following words:

The Panel recognizes that, in the final analysis, the most important determinants of audit effectiveness are the personal attributes and skills of the individual auditor. The personal attributes of individuals provide structure and definition for their role in society and establish the foundation for what constitutes a true professional. For the individual auditor, these attributes are independence in fact and in appearance, adherence to strong ethical standards, a great sense of personal integrity and the will to act objectively even in the face of intense pressures. Most importantly, individual auditors, as members of a respected profession, should assign their highest priority to protecting the public interest.

. . . auditors must possess the discipline, fortitude and ability to stand up to management or to an audit committee or board of directors. They need to be able to say, "No, that's not right!"

Critical to such discipline is firm management giving clear and consistent messages that it not only expects auditors to do the right thing, but also will support them, fully and unequivocally, when "no" is the right answer—even when that means losing a client.

Each and every auditing professional contributes to the performance of an audit. No amount of guidance, admonitions to do good work, the right "tone at the top," or the threat of sanctions will produce a high-quality audit, unless every individual auditor embraces a high sense of personal responsibility and diligence. The Panel calls on all individual professional auditors to heed this message. Only quality audits serve the public interest, and the public is your most important client.[2]

I believe the committee's concluding remarks are correct. There are no simple, "silver bullet" answers to our complex ethical crisis. But people desperately want a solution that's obvious, quick, and simple. Like, "don't let the auditors provide tax or consulting services." Or, "change the way we account for stock options." H.L. Mencken got it right years ago when he said, "There is an easy solution to every known problem—neat, plausible—and wrong!"

In the final analysis, the real problems seem to boil down to insufficient character and courage on the part of accountants and auditors to do the right thing in spite of the consequences. Management of clients and firms was also at fault for not providing adequate support systems and structures, including the "culture" and the ethical "tone at the top" to properly influence these weak individuals.

What if this assessment is right? What if the problems we face really aren't a function of whether auditors do consulting or tax work or how we account for stock options? What if they really are all about character and ethics and values, what do we do?

To make real progress, we first have to recognize that there is no simple or quick fix to the complex challenges we face. Once we abandon the seductive desire for a "quick fix," we must then accept the limited role that institutions such as government, regulators, corporations, oversight boards, auditing firms, and, yes, universities can effectively play in solving problems of ethics and integrity in our society and our capital markets.

That's not to say that institutions don't have a role—they do. An important role.

But, unpopular as this notion of personal responsibility is in our society, ethics, and integrity—or the lack of them—finally boils down to individual people and the decisions they make.

Perhaps T.S. Eliot said it best: "They constantly try to escape from the darkness outside and within—by dreaming of systems so perfect that no one will need to be good."

Well, like it or not, we do need to be good—individually—every day—day in and day out. We can't abdicate to institutions, policies, regulations, or laws our personal responsibility for integrity and ethical behavior. After all, it's irresponsible for us to expect others to behave better than we do. For example, when we're at work, what right do we have to expect our supervisors to treat us fairly, unless we personally treat those we supervise fairly? What right do we have to expect our children to behave better than we do?

The destruction of our ethical consensus was not the fault of our institutions. It was caused by the individuals in these institutions. And if we are able to rebuild an ethical consensus within the accounting and auditing profession and our society, it will happen because of the actions and behavior of individuals committed to doing the right things.

Consider the reaction to the accounting and auditing problems. Andersen has been destroyed by an indictment. Sarbanes-Oxley has been passed. The PCAOB (Public Company Accounting Oversight Board) has been created to oversee the auditing profession. Audit committees have established much closer working relationships with their auditors. Rating agencies and shareholder proxy organizations are taking much more aggressive positions on corporate governance issues. Regulators, attorneys general, and the trial bar are savaging the remaining audit firms.

What are the consequences to the accounting and auditing profession of all these reforms and reactions? As you might guess, the results are mixed.

The good news:

1. Company accountants and their auditors are taking their jobs much more seriously.
2. Senior managers at public companies are much more responsible in their approach to accounting, reporting, and auditing matters.
3. Audit committees are intensely focused on reporting matters, and their direct responsibility for the audit firm relationship is making auditors much more independent.
4. The quality of financial reporting has increased significantly.
5. The concept of control is much better understood among public companies and their auditors.
6. Directors are doing a much more responsible job of governance. More directors are independent of management and qualified to do their jobs. Meetings are longer and more frequent. Questions are more pointed and challenging. Management is being held accountable.

The bad news:

1. The reforms have been very expensive—many factors higher than ludicrous SEC estimates. There is no correlation between the cost of individual reforms and their benefits. Sec 404 is easily the most expensive, but the creation of independent audit committees and requiring management sign off on financials may have been the most effective reforms. As a consequence, auditors are now being criticized, even by regulators, for doing *too much work*.
2. Reducing auditor scope of services has significantly reduced access to critical competencies for audit teams, such as IT, evaluation, actuarial, tax, etc.
3. Audit firms are now subject to potential extortion by attorneys general. An auditing firm cannot fight for what they believe is right in a criminal investigation. They are dead as soon as they are indicted. So they must agree to virtually anything to avoid being indicted—pay huge fines, admit to crimes they didn't commit, and give up their partners for individual prosecution. Without regards to the merits of the recent KPMG investigation, they had no choice but to settle, even if they had done absolutely nothing wrong. This situation cannot be allowed to continue. The temptation for judicial overreaching is just too great.
4. Audit firms are being sued in private litigation for vast sums of money. The firms are basically uninsured in almost every case; the firm must agree to settle because an adverse decision could put them out of business.
5. The public's misconceptions about accounting and auditing have not changed. They still:
   - Believe financial statements are inherently precise or should be.
   - Don't understand the overwhelming complexity of financial reporting.
   - Believe that auditors have the ability to detect collusive fraud on a timely basis.

These misconceptions virtually guarantee a continuation of high-profile accounting and auditing "failures."

My conclusion is that much good has come from the so-called reforms. For example, I believe we are at a high watermark for financial reporting, with almost everyone making an intense effort to report fairly and honestly. On the other hand, I believe it is unlikely that the Big Four firms will survive, and I believe that will be a great loss to the capital formation system. Having been lost, the private audit firm model is probably not retrievable. I believe whatever replaces the Big Four is likely to be a far inferior product. For example, the GAO (General Accounting Office) is rumored to be preparing a contingency plan to replace the Big Four firms if they do not survive as auditors.

Another reason why I'm pessimistic about the future of auditing is the pervasive nature of the ethical decline across our society. Doing the politically easy thing has become a replacement for doing the responsible thing. It is difficult to imagine a politician or regulator or attorney general stepping up and defending the auditing profession when it is bound to be politically unpopular to do so. A perfect example is Andersen's demise. It should not have happened. It was not in the public's best interest. But our leaders were not willing to challenge public opinion.

This should warn us that the ethical crisis in our society has yet to be addressed. Financial reporting is better and will be for a while, but that is a small fraction of our total society. All of our basic institutions need reform, and those institutions will change for the better only when the behavior of the individuals who comprise them improves. Only by becoming more ethical people will we have a more ethical society.

Thank you for your attention. I believe groups like yours are part of the solution to our crisis, and I thank you very much for caring about ethics.

NOTES

1. Portions of this presentation contain quotations from "Ethics as an Imperative," by James E. Copeland, Jr., published in *Accounting Horizons*, 19, no. 1 (March 2005): 35–43. Copyright © American Accounting Association. The full text of this article is available online at http://aaahq.org/ic/browse.htm.

2. The Panel on Audit Effectiveness: Report and Recommendations, Public Oversight Board, August 31, 2000, xiv.

CHAPTER SEVEN

Integrity and Profits: Can Companies Have Both in a World Where Sex Sells?

Debra S. Waller
Chairman and CEO, Jockey International
June 22, 2004

> So in an age that celebrates diversity is my own diversity okay? Avoiding the "sex sells" approach?

Sit back and imagine the students at a particular all girls' college being allowed to go out only on Saturday night. But on a Tuesday evening a young man showed up and told the older woman in the dorm lobby that it was imperative that he see a certain girl immediately. The young man explained that he wanted to surprise her. "You see," he said, "I'm her brother." The woman replied, "Oh she'll be surprised all right. But think about how surprised I am. I'm her mother."

These days, it's almost hard to relate to a world like that. Dating permitted only on Saturday nights. In today's society it's almost a joke within itself. It's hard to believe that a college could have regulated the dating habits of students.

As business leaders, we all know we are living in a changing world. And I think we would generally agree that change is good. Selling as much underwear as we do at Jockey, we naturally believe in change. That's how it is with underwear.

But I don't think any of us wants to embrace *every* change. For example, the risqué performance during half time at the last Super Bowl was a big change. We also see change as we're waiting in the line at the grocery store facing magazine covers with increasingly mature themes—covers that can prompt conversations with our children or grandchildren that we wish could wait until they were older.

It often seems that everywhere we go we are confronted with another reminder of the tired marketing adage "sex sells." Because I'm in the underwear business, people sometimes ask me, "So Debra, is it true? Does sex really sell?" Of course the answer to this question is obvious. Yes sex does sell. Dating back to the world's oldest profession.

But I don't think people are really asking me for a literal answer. After all, the answer is so obvious. I think what they are really getting at is more subtle. They see that sex is used to sell just about everything, but they wonder if it really has to be that way because they are not comfortable with that.

So in an age that celebrates diversity is my own diversity okay? Avoiding the "sex sells" approach? Is it okay for my business to be different, or must I too follow the crowd to succeed? Perhaps I hear this so often because I work at an underwear company. One whose products are sold in over 120 countries around the world.

In my industry, some of the edgiest advertising you will ever see is designed without even showing underwear. For example, there are underwear ads where none of the models are wearing any underwear—or anything else for that matter. It's not surprising that many people assume that such might be the only thing that sells underwear.

But I am pleased to say there are alternatives—effective, bottom-line business alternatives. Alternatives that are reinforcing to human dignity and to personal ethics. There's an old saying that still holds true today: If you want to be a success in business find a need and meet it. And that's how our company got started back in 1876. Our founder, Samuel T. Cooper, a retired minister, met some lumberjacks whose lives and limbs were being threatened by, of all things, their socks. Hard to believe, right? That socks could be a problem. They were made out of shoddy wool and wore unevenly. Sometimes they would last for days and other times they would last for months. But the lumberjacks could never be sure, so when they least expected it a hole would develop—leading to a blister that could lead to an infection.

And in those days a common medical treatment was amputation. In an era without any social program, entire families could be crushed by such a physical impairment. It was a serious problem. Reverend Cooper had no intention of getting into the sock business, but he couldn't find high-quality socks for these lumberjacks elsewhere. So he assembled some ladies in his hometown to make better socks. As word spread, he was confronted with more demand than he ever anticipated. So Jockey International was founded all because he inadvertently found and met a human need.

One thing that hasn't changed since 1876 is that people still have needs and they always will. And they will still support companies that provide unique products or services to meet their unique, individual needs. Consumers are looking for businesses to improve their quality of life in whatever ways possible, big or small. So at Jockey that's why we focus on consumer needs.

Just a few years ago we were aware that fashion designers were turning back the clock. The 1970s were coming back strong. Complete with hip huggers and form-fitting fashion, and that created a new underwear need. Ladies, I know you can identify with this. Pantyline? Can we identify? And gentlemen, in case you don't know, that is a concern when we wear tight-fitting clothes. So we developed innovate intimates that we called the Jockey "No Pantyline Promise Collection." And it continues to be successful for us. We didn't need to use edgy marketing because we had something better that grabbed consumers' attention. We had a solution to their problem.

Now I don't need to be doing a commercial for Jockey but when people ask about Jockey's alternative to "sex sells," that's it. Innovative products that meet the human need for comfort. Now you may say, "But it's just underwear. It's a commodity. What could you possibly do to make it stand out from the crowd?" Please take my word for it; underwear does not have to be a commodity. It can be an innovative fashion item driven by consumers' needs. That's a universal concept regardless of the nature of your business. How about lettuce? Some people might be tempted to say that too is a commodity. What on earth could you do with lettuce that would be innovative and would boost sales? You can cut it up, put it in a bag with croutons and dressing, and call it a salad kit. It revolutionized the lettuce market. Somewhere a business leader was in touch with his consumers' needs—aware that consumers were stressed for time, aware that this time crunch was a horrible threat to the lettuce industry, and also aware that this could be an opportunity for an innovation that would meet the need.

And when it comes to successful marketing we've learned that it doesn't have to be edgy. In fact, our market research suggests that Jockey consumers are looking for the exact opposite: pure, simple, wholesome, and good. They want that which appeals to common sense. And while many companies have been considering this more in the post-9/11 world, we've found this to be consistently true throughout our history.

So we develop sophisticated advertisements that are soothing and nurturing. Advertisements that are congruent with what our consumers tell us that they want. Advertisements that are a reflection of our consumers. The settings are warm and peaceful. The models are confident and approachable not dark and gaunt.

We also pay attention to little details. Men and women in our ads routinely wear wedding rings. It's a small detail I know but consumers notice it. In fact, you might be surprised what our consumers notice and talk to us about. In our call center, we hear from over 100,000 consumers every year. Here's just what one of them wrote to us in an e-mail: "I was so relieved to see your ads. The man and the woman in the underwear both were wearing wedding rings. These days it's good to see a company that reaffirms that it's okay to be married. That there's nothing wrong with being married and that married people can be happy." And another one says, "There are other underwear brands in department stores. But yours is the one that most identifies with the values of my family, and that's one important reason why I buy Jockey."

According to the newspaper other companies are also considering softer, gentler approaches to their marketing. For example, *USA Today* reported in April that Abercrombie & Fitch, which regularly included nudity in its catalog, announced that it is toning down its publications. It is said that nudity will not be seen in this year's catalog.

Clearly there are many ways of doing business. At Jockey we have no intention of telling any other business what to do. But at the same time we're very comfortable with what we do and it works. It has since 1876. It resonates with our values. It serves our consumers. It sustains our economic health. At the same time we realize that not every business is operating on the same wavelength. We can't assume that the world around us is just like we are. There are so many different people out there working at different companies with different values. And we all have to work together.

Sometimes advertising isn't easy. Choosing magazines to advertise in is like walking a tightrope and I never claim that we make the perfect choice every time. But that's the world you and I have to live in—an imperfect world, a complex world that doesn't purposely harmonize with us all the time. So we control the things that we can control. And as a privately held company we do have more control over our destinies than many publicly held companies.

Nonetheless, I think that all of us share the potential to use our creativity and customer insight to carve out a unique path for our businesses. Many go the route of "sex sells," and certainly at Jockey we could too; but why be so narrow in our thinking? In a world of great diversity why would we want to be a cookie cutter clone? Why do so when many others are already doing the same thing? And why would we want to abandon an approach that has worked so well for us for so long. As a business leader I don't see a need to choose between ethics and corporate profit. Generation after generation our company has thrived by making sure that our own ethical compass points toward the true north. And we follow our customers.

We're not perfect. We've made mistakes. Sometimes we've veered off to one side or the other, but that's when we need to check the compass and that's when we make corrections, of course. It's not easy. And as some people have pointed out, it would probably be easier to choose between the high road to ethics and the quicker path to profit. But ultimately history teaches that the more challenging road is the more successful one.

For 128 years it has been so at Jockey. And I trust that it will continue to be so for Jockey—and for you and me personally.

CHAPTER EIGHT

The Moral Basis of Competitiveness

Karen Katen
Vice Chairman, Pfizer Inc., and President of Pfizer Human Health
November 30, 2005

> I can understand why the public's concerned with the cost—and confused by the value—of finding and using new medicines. America spends a lot of money on fighting disease, and every day we spend more.

"The Moral Basis of Competitiveness." That does sound pretty heavy. But if you're bracing yourself for another sermon on the wonders of the free market, I guess the good news and bad news is that it's not that simple.

Just like there are no atheists in foxholes, there are no market theorists in hospital beds. No one in the emergency room reads Adam Smith for comfort, although they may for anesthetic purposes.

But people do turn to the market for "the blessings forthcoming when our science determines what disease is, how it works, and how it may be cured." And prevented.

If you define business morality as "work based on principles that support ethical outcomes," there is, in fact, a moral element to the mission on your "Gravity Monument."

But that doesn't make it easy or simple to talk about. Trying to find moral clarity in the vexing complexity of our healthcare system can bring out the skeptic in all of us.

Healthcare is arguably the most-complicated and -regulated endeavor in the world—a field that mixes the oil and water of medicines and markets, a business that exists to do well *and* do good through work that by nature insinuates itself into people's most-personal fears and hopes.

No wonder we see contradictions—and high emotions—everywhere we look. The same Congressman who berates pharmaceutical companies on the House floor one minute . . . the next minute picks up the phone and calls our offices to find our best new cutting-edge clinical trial because a loved one was just diagnosed and needs help.

Fair enough—we're happy to help anyone we can.

I mean it. I'm convinced that a huge percentage of those who work in our sector are drawn by a moral mission and deeply believe that there's more purpose to work than just to make money.

I'll go a step further: If you think "the business of business is simply business," I think maybe you shouldn't be in business at all. In the long run, the market won't support you—and neither will your own people.

To be moral in a market-based healthcare company, you need people who treat shareholders with *respect*, patients with *compassion*, and disease with *fierce aggression*.

Disease is our competition.

Let me point out that my speech title today isn't "the moral basis of competition." It's "the moral basis of *competitiveness*." That means *readiness* to take on the good fight.

So to be competitive in this field means being ready to take on the enemy— disease. That enemy is what gives our work a moral component. And to take on disease effectively means running a tight, solid business, being fearless around risk, and doing well to do good.

That is particularly true today. Professor Lynn Sharp Paine of Harvard Business School writes, "Contrary to theorists who for centuries declared the corporation to be an amoral creature, society today has endowed the corporation with a moral personality."

Today, you have to start from moral questions in doing business. Competitiveness has to be based on moral concern and honorable action—in general, I believe—and particularly in the field of health.

So yes, of course, the people of Pfizer are happy to help when we get those calls from people who need help with their health . . . even calls from our critics. In fact, *especially* from our critics—because when we get those calls, it tells us that deep down, even some of our harshest detractors fundamentally trust our work.

That's the moral basis of competition: Trust. Trust comes from credibility, and credibility comes from consistent and authentic moral behavior.

You cannot compete without trust. But you can't fake it or buy it. You have to deserve it.

To do that, every company, every industry, has to fulfill a social contract that lies at the crosshairs of some human passions. In our line of work, those crosshairs are health and money. People deserve the first and earn the second—so they consider both of them rights. That's their starting point, and they find the concept of having to pay for a right morally problematic.

In fact, the very idea of for-profit healthcare can offend deep sensibilities embedded in almost every culture. For thousands of years, selflessly helping the sick has been a paradigm of moral behavior. Buddha, Mohammad, and Lord Ram tended the sick, the old and the feeble. The mitzvah of bikkur cholim, or visiting the ill, is a major tenet of observant Judaism. Jesus healed the sick and defended the weak.

These are our models of moral behavior, and their influence runs very deep. That's why, for centuries, most money for healthcare research—and nearly all money for hospitals and other large healthcare facilities—came from charities, religious organizations, and the public purse. A century ago, physicians weren't even allowed to charge for their services to patients in hospitals, and the AMA has long taken a very dim view of doctors competing on price.

So Adam Smith's clear proposition of the invisible hand gets murky when you put a third-party payer into the mix, and murkier still when you throw in the idea of profit.

People accept that while they may need a car, they don't have a right to a Cadillac. But they *do* believe they deserve Cadillac healthcare.

It's understandable. All of us want the best-possible care for ourselves and our loved ones—and we'll fight for it.

We also tend to equate good healthcare with expensive healthcare, and we want a Cadillac, even though a Camry would get us where we're going just as well. As patients, we see disengaged, rational economic models as irrelevant. We lead from the heart, not the head.

As patients, we aren't interested in the cycle of risk and reward that science drives through markets to improve the quality of health. We're interested in being well. That's what patients need.

Now, when you provide something people truly need, they're grudgingly grateful—but that "grudge" can be profound. Psychologists call it "dependency resentment," and it can stand in the way of trust.

A recent *New York Times Magazine* article illustrates the problem. It tells about the author's son, whose life is being restored by a new medicine. Here's how the father ends the story:

I do not have the luxury of distrust.
    I do not love drugs.
I do not love the companies that sell them.
    But I do love my son.

The medicine that's giving this man's son back to him has significant R&D costs; it didn't just fall out of the sky; so I wish he'd used the word "discover" medicines instead of just "sell" them. I also wished he liked us. But that's not a moral issue.

The real moral issue—what really bothers me about this story—is the fact that he's uneasy with granting us trust—although he needs to. That's terrible.

What can we, in the pharmaceutical sector, do to deserve and earn the trust of that father, and millions of others who feel the same way? Well, we could be rational and explain our world in terms of those two crosshairs—health and money.

Let's start with health.

Consider that you and I now live eight days a week. That's true in the United States, compared to our grandparents a half-century ago. They lived about sixty-eight years. An American born today should live to be about seventy-seven. So if you take 1950 as a baseline in terms of a seven-day week, today, every week, you and I have an extra day to live—thanks to advances in healthcare, generally, and disproportionately thanks to pharmaceuticals, specifically. We all die of something, but most of the major infectious diseases that loomed over our grandparents are now either greatly reduced or gone.

Food for thought. But does it change your heart when your child is sick? No.

Okay, so let's talk about money. Why do medicines cost so much? Because discovering them is risky and hard.

Most of Pfizer's 10,000 research and development scientists work an entire career and never touch a compound that becomes an actual medicine. That's costly. We spend $22 million daily on research and development—almost a million dollars every hour, around the clock, every working day.

We're investing nearly $800 million in just one clinical trial for just one potential new medicine to raise "good" cholesterol, which could possibly extend millions of lives. That's a huge financial risk, considering we don't even know if the medicine will ever make it to FDA review, much less be approved.

In fact, only one in 15,000 new compounds we synthesize for further study . . . ever makes it to patients. The one that does could take fifteen years and $1.5 billion to develop, and only one out of three that make it to patients ever recovers its costs.

Does that mean we're squandering money, chasing therapeutic rabbits down their holes? No—it means we're following the scientific method. We *have* to chase rabbits because one might be the one to cure cancer—and we can't know which one it will be.

But that means we also have to be efficient. Pfizer has the world's largest molecular library—which you might think would fit on the head of a pin, but it's actually a very large operation, using high-throughput screening that can fly through hundreds of millions of possible compounds in world-class time.

It's risky and costly—but it works. Discovery comes before development, and right now, we have more than 400 research programs looking into potential new areas of discovery.

Take the next step, and we have 220 distinct research programs evaluating 140 New Molecular Entities in development—compounds well on their way to becoming potential new medicines, including some lifesaving advances against cancer.

Considering the high failure rate of chasing medicinal rabbits, and the high costs of discovery and development—like the $800 million clinical trial I mentioned—it's clear why finding new medicines is a risky and expensive proposition.

It's true that the second pill may cost a dollar to make, but the first may cost a billion.

So yes, new medicines require staggering investments. Interesting facts—but do they change hearts? No.

Okay, so we could take a third approach and talk about where health and money intersect, and suggest that for any society, health equals wealth. Studies from Stanford, Berkeley, the University of Chicago, and other institutions show that the cost of new medicines pays back dollars on pennies, in savings and productivity. One in particular, from Columbia University, shows that a dollar spent on a new medicine instead of an older therapy ends up saving seven dollars down the road.

All this sounds very interesting. But does it change hearts? Does it build trust? Read the headlines. The answer is no.

Fair enough. I can understand why the public's concerned with the cost—and confused by the value—of finding and using new medicines. America spends a lot of money on fighting disease, and every day we spend more.

This causes concern for Americans, and it causes problems for pharmaceuticals, because when you look for someone to blame, you look for what you can see. Even experts can't see very clearly into our opaque healthcare system, but everyone sees prescription copayments go up—and they naturally assume pharmaceutical companies are the main culprits.

But are we?

Well, first of all, we don't determine copays. Insurers and payers do. More to the point, prescriptions account for about the same 10 percent of total U.S. healthcare costs as they did forty years ago—a dime for every healthcare dollar.

In terms of actual costs, almost three-quarters of the rise in prescription spending is because medicines are being used more often, and very often they're used to keep a chronic condition from getting worse to the point of requiring surgery or causing death.

The truth is, the bulk of rising healthcare spending doesn't come from prescriptions. It comes from diagnostic devices and surgical techniques. Goldman Sachs estimates these two factors account for more than half the rise of total U.S. healthcare costs over the past three years.

But patients don't see these costs.

One of our Pfizer colleagues made a recent speech to a group of elderly patients. He asked how many had had joint-replacement surgery. Almost every hand went up. He asked how many were upset at the cost. Almost every hand went down.

Then he asked how many took a prescription. Every hand went up. He asked how many were upset at the cost. Almost every hand stayed up.

Why? Because they never saw the $40,000 bill for their surgery, but they saw that prescription copay creep up from five to ten to fifteen dollars.

So we're back where we started. Hard numerical arguments don't work. To make progress on this issue, we need a fundamental shift in our thinking.

We should be looking not at cost but at cost-effectiveness. We should be looking at the value of health and the cost of disease, not just the price of medicines. We should be looking at better health outcomes—at better results.

That's the moral question—how to get good health results. Isn't that what the market wants? Isn't that what we should deliver?

Peter Drucker thought so. You know he passed away this month, and his obituary in the *Economist* said this about him:

Drucker was too sensitive to the thin crust of civilization to share the classic liberal faith in the market, but too clear-sighted to embrace the growing fashion for big-government solutions. He told his clients, including the American Red Cross and the Girl Scouts of America, that they needed to deal in "changed lives," not just maximum profits. But he also warned that the market would judge them not on the goodness of their intentions, but on the basis of their results.[1]

This very smart man had a sign outside his office that read: "What is our business? Who is our customer? What does the customer value?"

These aren't just practical questions. They're questions about addressing what people need from you, and in good faith ask of you—and that makes them moral questions.

Because of the gravity of answers people expect of us, I submit that with full understanding, the market would say that a pharmaceutical sector that isn't competitive is downright immoral.

How do we answer Drucker's questions? What does society want from us? How do we use the power of the market to deliver?

Being a moral business means doing the right thing—like adding an extra day of life to our week. But part of it also means making things right when you've done something wrong. It means changing to fix a problem that you've helped cause.

I can think of at least five major changes our company or industry has recently made to correct problems that trouble our stakeholders.

First, people are frightened and angry when they can't afford their medicines. In the United States, almost 500 programs exist to help, but they're confusing and people don't use them. So this year, our industry association, PhRMA, created a one-stop clearinghouse—a one-call hotline—to help people sort through all the discount-medicine programs. You call an 800 number and talk to a real person who asks questions and determines the best program for you, including programs for the poor, and for uninsured people with good incomes, to get medicines at deep discounts or even for free.

Second, people are angry about our advertising. They say it trivializes medicine, infantilizes patients, and drives up our prices. The third complaint isn't true—if anything, in fact, it drives them down—but I'll concede the first two with a sincere mea culpa. We're new to consumer advertising, as you may know—until a few years ago we weren't allowed to do it. So we've made mistakes and we've learned.

You know you've arrived when *The Simpsons* TV show makes fun of you. Well, now apparently little Lisa is suffering from "disappointment disorder."

Point taken. But we know for a fact—and doctors do, too—that advertising does save lives by sending patients to doctors. We just need to do it better. Our advertising should be highly educational, not purely promotional.

So we've reformed our industry advertising guidelines. Our new ads will use plainer language to talk about risks, encourage patients to talk with their doctors, and follow medical instructions. We'll also hold off on advertising any new medicine to the public for at least six months, so healthcare providers will have time to learn how it works.

Pfizer has gone a step further and decided to treat health as a standalone "brand." We've allotted roughly the same budget we'd normally apply to advertising a major medicine, and we'll apply it to ad campaigns that don't mention a medicine at all. Instead, they'll promote health, through prevention, diet, exercise, a strong patient–doctor relationship and compliance with doctors' instructions.

Third, doctors are frustrated with visits from too many pharmaceutical reps. They need and appreciate the information these reps provide—doctors don't have time to keep up with the latest, and our reps are true experts—but they asked us for fewer and shorter visits. So we reorganized and retrained our medical-marketing sales forces this year so they don't compete with each other—and more important, don't compete with patients waiting for the doctor's time. This was a very disruptive and costly change, but it's enlightened self-interest to make painful changes when your customer tells you they're needed.

Fourth, patients are bewildered by healthcare—by our system on one hand, which is horrendously hard to navigate, and by a language of medicine they don't understand. So helping people navigate the system and understand the vernacular is crucial, and we're developing programs to advance both causes. Early results show our approach is quantifiably effective, so we'll continue to invest in this area.

And finally, fifth, payers—insurers and governments—are crying for help to get better results from their spending, in terms of both health and costs. So we've put into practice what we know to be true: If you focus entire health systems on improving outcomes, you don't just get healthier patients—you get smaller medical bills. We've proven it on a very large scale to the state of Florida—with help from Matria Healthcare through a program called "A Healthy State" and we're applying the same model around the world and also within our own company. The outcomes show that you *can* improve health and cut costs at the same time. In fact, one naturally follows the other.

Each of these five issues is the tip of its own moral iceberg, and our solutions are practical. But they're not nearly enough. Healthcare is big, and healthcare is broken. Its problems are larger than any one sector can address alone, and we need all parties involved to help fix it. It's going to take a national effort—actually a worldwide effort, across industries and governments. We need to find common social standards regarding health that we all can agree are moral—including issues of affordability, access, education, resources, and health outcomes. We have to do this work together if we're going to make healthcare right for everyone.

All this goes to Drucker's approach: Ask what the customer considers value, and respond to provide it. Fix problems you've caused, but go further. If it requires working in tandem with others to do the right thing for society at large—even without profit—do what you can there, too.

Of course we need to make profit, or all is lost. We're responsible to shareholders as well as to patients. But if Drucker is right, the first group will be served if we serve the second. And if Drucker is right, it's not just good business, but the right thing to do, to help those who can't help themselves when you can. That's why we take corporate citizenship very seriously.

While we don't talk about it much, for fear it would cheapen our efforts, we *are* gratified when we're able to help victims of natural disasters or disease who aren't able to help themselves.

It goes to the intrinsic nature of the type of people that I believe are attracted to pharmaceutical work. They want to do *well*, of course. But they also want to do *good*.

Every year, when we open enrollment for our "Global Health Fellows," which is kind of like a rotating Peace Corps program we developed to send colleagues to pockets of need around the world, the flood of applications is overwhelming. When those participants come back from a tour overseas, they bring back new perspectives on what needs have to be met.

That's valuable to Pfizer, and to our constituencies, because the most-noble claim of market theory is that where there's a need, the market will find a way to meet it.

"Finding a way" is the tough part. Helping one constituency sometimes hurts another. How does a company find moral clarity among such complexities?

For my sector, I think our homing point—our touchstone that makes everything clear—is really pretty simple. *Honor the science to serve the patient.* Do that one thing, and you can't help but make real progress and build trust in the process.

Regarding progress, let me leave you with one last statistic.

I went to the University of Chicago Graduate School of Business, affectionately known as "Quantitative U." Two economists there conclude that if the United States can cut death by cancer by 20 percent over the next ten years, our economy would get a boost to the tune of $10 trillion.

That's a one with a dozen zeroes behind it.

The nobility behind that staggering figure isn't economic. It's the human story behind the number. People not just being productive, but spending time with loved ones.

That's a moral goal, and to walk away from it would be downright immoral.

It's not a question of trading money for health. If we get this right, we won't have to pay one for the other. We'll get both.

The end game is this: Adding years to life and life to years. We have compounds in our pipeline that can help—and so do other fine companies.

Will we support the science that fuels that pipeline? Will we make the same moral choice that our grandparents made a half-century ago?

They could've said, "Seven days a week—that's plenty." Instead, they asked—"Why not eight?"

Shouldn't we ask—"Why not nine?"

I believe the moral answer is *yes*.

NOTE

1. "Peter Drucker, "Trusting the Teacher in the Grey-Flannel Suit: The One Management Thinker Every Educated Person Should Read," *The Economist*, November 17, 2005 (accessed online at http://www.economist.com).

CHAPTER NINE

Excellence without a Soul? Higher Education and the Shaping of Moral Character

Harry R. Lewis
Professor and Former Dean of Harvard College
December 8, 2006

> We owe it to society to see that the future business leaders, government leaders we produce will learn that their role in life is about something bigger than themselves and their personal success.

It's a pleasure and an honor to be here. I have heard so many times in recent years about the need for universities to be more businesslike that I am humbled that people from the world of business affairs would want to hear from me and other university leaders. There are, of course, some important ways in which universities *are* businesses, and there are some equally important differences. I'd like to talk for a bit about institutional mission and about the pursuit of excellence. I'm going to talk about how mission and the pursuit of excellence are connected, and how ethical principles can get compromised when ambitions for excellence make us lose sight of our mission.

I come to this as a higher ed lifer; except for a couple of years in government service right after I got out of college, I have barely left Harvard. I'd like to make some observations, on the basis of this long perspective, about what has happened in higher education, in part, as a result of the competitive pursuit of excellence and, in part, as a result of imperatives for universities to become more businesslike. Universities have always been thought somewhat ridiculous for their inefficiency; it *can* take a long time to develop a consensus on anything in a university, and the less consequential the decision, the more time committees can spend deliberating it. As the political scientist Wallace Sayre once said, "In any dispute the intensity of feeling is inversely proportional to the value of the stakes at issue—that is why academic politics are so bitter." (An idea not original with Henry Kissinger, it turns out.) I think we sometimes use the same decision-making methods for buying furniture as we do for things that are really hard, such as defining our curriculum. And furniture might well be better chosen autocratically. But figuring out what the common core requirements for an undergraduate degree should be is an institutional identity search, not something that should be done on a deadline. Properly done, it is a sort of collective psychoanalysis. But I am getting ahead of my story.

The idea that a university should even *have* a mission used to strike me as odd. Harvard College didn't have one until the late '90s—the late 1990s, I mean! Writing one was one of my odder jobs as dean. The reason I had to write a mission statement for Harvard College was because the NCAA came to accredit our athletic program, and the first accreditation standard was to ensure that the mission of the athletic department was consistent with the mission of the university. When we told the green eye shades from the NCAA that Harvard *had* no mission statement, they didn't believe us, and insisted that we couldn't be a *real* college without one. We produced both mission statements for them, the one for the College and the one for the Athletic Department. But we felt rather like the department store customer who has his credit card returned to him so he can sign the card before the store will accept it. You know, the clerk then dutifully compares the signature on the card to the signature on the charge slip and confirms that they are identical. Our two missions did turn out to be consistent, and we were accredited.

I don't like the exercise of mission statements, because they tend to wind up with everything in them, including the kitchen sink, even if you aren't really in the kitchen sink business. An honest mission statement is falsifiable; you should be able to decide *not* to do something because it isn't part of your mission.

So what *is* the mission of a university? Teaching and research, people usually say in so many words. And to be sure, all professors teach and we all do research, or are supposed to. But it's really both less and more than that. *Education*, I'd say, not teaching; and mostly *education of the young*. The Office of Civil Rights would probably not let us say "education of the young," because it would be age-discriminatory, but that is the most important thing we do: turn eighteen-year-olds into twenty-two-year-olds to whom we can confidently turn over responsibility for society once we old folks are done with it. Just *what* we teach in order to fulfill our educational mission is hugely important, but one thing seems clear to me: Our job is not just to let students learn anything they want. That's why curricula are important, because defining a curriculum involves defining what it means to be educated. The significance of that goes back to Plato:

Youth is the time when the character is being molded and easily takes any impress one may wish to stamp on it. Shall we then simply allow our children to listen to any stories that anyone happens to make up and so receive into their minds ideas often the very opposite to those we shall think they ought to have when they are grown up?

I like that quotation, in its stilted translation and all, because it is the opening epigram in Harvard's greatest curricular report, the Red Book of 1945, officially known as *General Education in a Free Society*. One of the conclusions to which the Red Book came, looking across the oceans toward the smoldering ashes of German and Japan, was that part of education was learning the responsibilities of citizenship in a democracy. That role for higher education has largely been lost. Most universities seem to take it for granted that democracy will somehow survive no matter what, and our job is to critique it and to improve it, not to teach our students where it came from and what about it is fragile and why it is important.

In fact, the faculties of most universities, mine included, have a hard time with the idea that they have *any* kind of collective responsibility for the educational welfare of the entire student body, any collective educational mission. Instead, what we teach has become specialized and fragmented.

Students and their families do not see this as necessarily a bad thing. Universities are attending to a perversion of the business imperative: our students are our customers and should be given what they want. The curriculum should be a shopping mall. There should be options, and colors, and sizes, and features to choose among. We should give students the freedom to make those choices, and we should do so proudly.

The emptiness of our curricular structure legitimizes pettiness and triviality of students' concerns. Professors complain that students are too materialistic, too preprofessional, like sports too much, and don't respect the life of the mind. But it's our own damn fault; we are so focused on our specialized expertise that we haven't given students a good enough reason to think that ideas are important to them, or to think that there are any big lessons they might gain from their education that are more significant than their pursuit of pleasure and success and money and fame.

Freedom as a value is hard to argue against; I sound slightly ridiculous when I tell people that I'm antifreedom, as far as students go, and therefore procoercion, I guess. In truth, student freedom is popular in universities because it works well for faculty as well as for students.

Why is the unstructured curriculum so attractive to faculty? Because it goes nicely with our success with the other piece of our mission, research. Now I think just saying "research" is as misleading as just saying "teaching." I'd be inclined to be a bit more specific. Not just any research, but the preservation of the learning of the past and the production of knowledge that promises to be of significance to society in the future. The notion that our research function is in some vague way tied to societal benefit seems to me more consistent with the tax exemptions universities receive. It's also more consistent with our historical mission, in this country at least.

Harvard was America's first university, and it was founded because the Puritans, a pretty well educated group, were terrified that the continent would be left illiterate once they were gone. Once they had taken care of the bare necessities of life, a Puritan author wrote, "one of the next things we longed for and looked after was to advance learning and perpetuate it to posterity; dreading to leave an illiterate ministry to the churches, when our present ministers shall lie in the dust." The thrust of that sentence is about illiteracy, not irreligion; in those days it went without saying that the only way to preserve literacy was through the ministers. Compare this to today. A recently released report states that *more than half of the graduates* from a *pretty good* list of colleges today think that nothing in the U.S. Constitution would prevent the establishment of a state religion in this country. I worry that with all the successes of our universities, sixty years after the Red Book we may be leaving the country illiterate in a different way.

What does research success have to do with the unstructured curriculum? The past fifty years have been a period of extraordinary growth and achievement for research universities. The knowledge they have created has propelled the American economy. All for the good. Diseases have been cured and Internets have been invented (claims by a former U.S. Senator notwithstanding). And as the rewards and glamour for universities shifted to research productivity, so did the incentive and reward structure for the faculty. One part of our mission dominated the other.

Of course we know we are in the education business too, so we have redefined education as teaching the specialized subjects we individually know and love. We use customer satisfaction surveys—excuse me, student course evaluations— to show we care about education. And once the customers are asked what they want—and students are involved in curricular decision-making in most universities now—it turns out that what they want most is freedom. Fewer required courses, less curricular structure, more ability to design their education for themselves.

They and their families certainly don't want to be told that the students are wrong, or are naughty people sometimes, or any of the other developmentally healthy things colleges used to talk about to young people. A college education is an expensive credential, after all. The customer is always right, and the customer is not paying for a credential with black marks on it. While I was dean I occasionally exasperated people by saying I am not only against *freedom* for students, I am also against *happiness*. Now I don't actually believe that students should be in *constant* misery, but students who live their entire lives, from age eighteen to twenty-two, in a state of constant happiness could not have learned much about themselves in college. "Know thyself " is still something worth shooting for, as an ambition for our students, and that can't happen unless their beliefs and their self-image are challenged rather than constantly indulged. If we don't challenge them, they are likely to crash at age twenty-five when they realize they have just been executing some program for life which they got from their parents and their TV shows.

Why don't we any more want to take on the troublesome task of real education? In the great research universities, the demands for freedom are easy to rally around. The faculty, eager to teach within their specialties, like less structure as much as the students do. If you are an expert in twelfth-century Chinese porcelain, there is little risk of being forced to take time away from that, in order to learn twentieth-century expressionist painting, for example, if your department doesn't even teach the art survey courses for which you might have to know that. So all the incentives and rewards are for specialized excellence in the faculty and the development of the same in students.

Deans and presidents become heroes to their students if they promise to liberate them from the shackles of curricular requirements. We are part of the American culture of fame, and universities just don't get famous for education. As a business it is all working perfectly—the customers are happy, the research product keeps improving, and we are constantly in the newspapers and on TV. And yet society—which helps to pay the bills through the tax exemptions it gives us—is not really getting its end of the bargain. In the last Massachusetts election, three out of the four candidates were Harvard graduates. Listening to the debates, I am more persuaded than ever that we need to do a better job teaching the lessons of history and our responsibility to look out for the best interests of society, however well we are teaching students in their majors.

Something else happens when a narrow slice of our mission dominates the whole, and faculty are hired and rewarded on the basis of scholarly excellence and ability to make the customers happy. We stop worrying about the character of the faculty, about whether they are the kind of people we actually want educating our children. Again I'm using education in the developmental sense, not just the information-transfer sense. My colleague Luke Menand in the English department said it compellingly: "*We* are the books our students read most closely." Shouldn't we care whether professors are good people, whether we should trust them to help our nineteen-year-olds figure out their lives and to set a good example for students when their activities are publicly visible? Every university I know does some kind of character evaluation when it hires athletic coaches; I know of none that does so when hiring professors. Why is that?

Universities abandoned character tests on the faculty in service of not one but two good intentions. One I have already talked about, the ambition for extreme scholarly excellence. That required an end to cronyism and patronism in faculty appointments. The other is our fear of our own odious institutional history of discrimination. In a business that is full of subjective judgments, the way to avoid the kind of anti-Semitism and discrimination against women and gays that used to be part of the hiring conversations is to hire only on the basis of scholarly brilliance and (to some degree) classroom teaching. (Or at least, to claim that that is the way we hire faculty.)

But at some level, this can't possibly make sense. Being smart is *not* the only thing that counts. Isn't it important that a professor can look a student in the eyes and see what cards he is holding, as the Kenny Rogers song says? Or have some humane instincts about what to do when a student breaks down crying in her office? And when every professional school now teaches ethics courses, don't colleges have some responsibility to teach, and to model, ethical behavior? Winning is not the only thing.

We at Harvard have had plenty of opportunity to think about these issues lately. For several years we have been watching the interesting case of Andrei Shleifer. Shleifer is an academic superstar, winner of the international prize for the top economist under forty, and a tenured member of our Economics Department. His tale has been laid out in an article in *Institutional Investor* and also in David Warsh's economics blog.

Shleifer headed a Harvard project that was supposed to help the new Russian state set up a free-market economy. While he was at it, he and members of his family made self-serving investments in Russia that violated any common-sense standard about conflicts of interest. The people of the United States brought charges against Harvard, Shleifer, and several others, claiming that Shleifer's acts violated U.S. code as well.

Harvard could have settled the case quickly, but instead it dragged on for years because Shleifer refused to admit he had done anything wrong and because Harvard did not divide the case and leave Shleifer to fend for himself. In fact, in the middle of the investigation, Harvard promoted Shleifer to a named chair after the President urged the dean of the Faculty to make sure Shleifer did not get lured away to another university.

In the end, a federal court found that Shleifer had conspired to defraud the government. Harvard was fined $26.5 million as a result. That number does not include legal fees, which were very high, and the cost of settling a related private civil suit.

Shleifer paid a $2 million fine of his own, denying to the end he had done anything wrong or had any regrets. He said he simply ran out of resources to fight the government.

Most of Shleifer's economist colleagues gathered around him supportively. One senior economist at Harvard said in the student newspaper, "We think about him not as the guy who was involved in the ... lawsuit—we think about him as the exciting, intellectually active colleague that we've always known." In fact, no one seems ashamed of this affair at all. The most regret any economist has expressed to me is that it is all too bad since it may cost Shleifer the Nobel Prize. Shleifer lost his named chair recently, but that was the same penalty delivered to another economics professor who had been arrested for stealing a truckload of horse manure. (I kid you not. Some people found it hard to believe there was not enough in the economics department already. But I digress.) Shleifer is now back in the classroom after taking a sabbatical. While some of us were calling for Harvard to say what, if anything, it had done to Shleifer, one of his colleagues stated derisively that he seems "quite content.... does not appear to have been whipped, beaten, tortured, or starved."

Now what does all this have to do with the day-to-day life of the university? It sets a moral tone, or rather, an amoral tone. *Our students will live up* to the expectations we set for them. Remember what Plato said: "Youth is the time when the character is being molded and easily takes any impress one may wish to stamp on it." So what happened? In the same *Crimson* story in which the Economics professor said that he and his colleagues did not think of Shleifer as the guy who conspired to defraud the government, an undergraduate who studied under Shleifer said, "He is an excellent professor and does remarkable research and those to me are the two main criteria that you should be using in deciding whether or not he's going to be a valued professor. The other stuff, that is for other people to worry about."

So there we are. Only connect. Is the other stuff for other people to worry about?

I meant a lot of different things by my title, *Excellence without a soul*. But certainly part of it is that the other stuff is for *us* to worry about. We had a similar situation with a student last year. She was caught plagiarizing large parts of a novel she'd written; the story was all over the newspapers. She seems to have suffered no consequences from Harvard, because she wasn't doing the novel for *Harvard*. That too, in Harvard's eyes, was apparently for other people to worry about. Harvard's business was limited to her term papers.

We owe it to society to see that the future business leaders, government leaders, lawyers, doctors, and teachers we produce will learn that their role in life is about something bigger than themselves and their personal success. Or at least, if they have the good fortune to have learned those values at home, we should not unteach them during the years they are in our care. If we don't do that job, then we should be held accountable for the white collar crimes, the political corruptions, and the corporate scandals in which our graduates get involved.

So I'll finish where I started. Universities are slow places for a reason. I hope that ongoing efforts to speed them up do not create a kind of quarterly report myopia about results. Universities need the support, the love, and *also* the critical oversight of those outside the academy. The real success of a university has to be measured by its impact on society on a time scale of decades. We have to teach our students their responsibility to see that their heirs enjoy the same freedoms of thought and action that we are privileged to enjoy. Getting those lessons across to young people requires valuing some aspects of human character to which we now pay only lip service, such as selflessness and compassion and humility. These are things which our system of incentives for hiring and promoting faculty does a lot to ignore and even to discourage. The relentless pursuit of fame, fortune, and excellence has turned the philosophy of the academy from altruism to egoism. I hope our real customers, not the students but the society into which they graduate, will hold us to a standard of success larger than our annual productivity. We all have a stake in seeing that universities fulfill their real mission.

PART III

Leadership and Ethics in Organizations

CHAPTER TEN

Building Trust in Trying Times

Gerald Grinstein
Chairman and CEO, Delta Air Lines
April 18, 2005

> When you pick up a newspaper and see that the CEO of X Company made $38 million . . . there is a growing feeling that the separation between the management level and the working level is to the disadvantage of employees. It seems to me it would be very hard to lead a company like that. And I don't think I could.

The CEO is really only a stand-in for the people he or she works with. So I want you to know that our employees are the backbone of this company, and we wouldn't be here today if it were not for the efforts that they're putting in during a challenging time.

The theme of my remarks today is trust. And when I think about it as one who has been a CEO of a number of companies, I've always said that the test of whether you should do something—or not do something—is how it would look if it appeared in the morning newspaper. The truth of the matter is that it is easy to confuse honesty with trust, and those two can be very different things. That is one of the things I have come to learn in the last several years.

When you deal with trust, you're dealing with something much more complicated. Take the example of a board of directors. In the past, the courts would generally uphold any actions that a board of directors took if it fulfilled their business judgment. Now the courts have started peeling back what they mean by business judgment, and what I'm seeing is that they now say you have a duty to go forward and ask questions. You have a duty to make yourself informed. You have a duty not to accept what people say without questioning it. You've got to vote it. And those are changes that have taken place over a short period of time.

I know the business community is uncomfortable with some of this and complains to a great extent about the burdens of cost and time and resources that must be committed to fulfilling Sarbanes-Oxley. But the new perspective of the courts and government regulators was a very natural reaction to what was taking place in the business community, where a whole series of events brought about a loss of trust.

I think it's a healthy development. I think it's appropriate and much more transparent to make the board's activities a focus of scrutiny. I really have less trouble with it than maybe some of my colleagues at other companies.

But there is another thing that is becoming much more important: the potential for personal liability of board members. At WorldCom recently, the directors had to settle beyond the insurance limits—that is, with their personal funds—because of the acts, or failures to act, as WorldCom was committing fraud. And I suspect that you are going to see more and more of that, where public officials demand personal responsibility, both at a civil and a criminal level, for the acts of corporate directors. I think that is a healthy development.

I happen to know the chairman of the audit committee at Enron. He was a former Dean of the Stanford Business School. He was an accountant—maybe one of the most famous and renowned accountants of that period of time. A Chief Financial Officer, Andy Fastow, comes to the board and says that he wants to set up a special-purpose entity, and that he wants to do countertrading with the company, and that he wants to suspend the ethics code of the company in order to do it. It doesn't seem to me that that is a time when you would automatically say, "Well that sounds all right, just go ahead with it." How much will the CFO be paid—$30 million—to bet against the company? It seems it would immediately raise questions about what was going on.

The duty to ask such questions is what it's all about now. And I think that as we go on you will see that will evolve in a healthy way. So it's not simply a matter of honesty, it's not simply a matter of exercising business judgment on what you know. As a director you have a duty to go beyond that. And protecting trust means you have a duty to more than honesty. The truth of the matter is that you must ask, what kind of constituency do I have out there. How do I have to behave with respect to them? What do I expect from them as we go ahead? And with trust, we're dealing with something that is very fragile.

I don't know whether many of you have seen the play by Andrew Lloyd Webber called *The Aspect of Love*. It examines love in all its relationships, not necessarily romantic love but love in a variety of ways. As we peel the love onion, we begin to see what we're trying to get at. You can look at trust the same way.

What I'd like to do is just talk a little bit about the past and give some examples from our lives at Delta, because we're a pretty good example of it. Delta, being in the airline industry, may be a company where a special kind of relationship is expected. Let me just identify a couple of reasons for this. One, of course, is safety. Every time you climb on board the plane, you have to have the confidence that it's well maintained, that the people who are flying it are skilled, that the people who are dealing with you are going to treat you with respect and dignity, and that nothing is going to be compromised. So there's that fundamental piece of trust that extends from our passengers to our employees. Safety is an obligation that we can't just assume, and we don't. The outside public has to accept that we are providing that, and they do. They trust us. That is something we have to work very hard to earn.

But there are other aspects of our business that also are subject to trust. I have always thought of Delta as kind of a commune. I'm not sure that any airline is very different but there's always been a special relationship inside Delta. It goes back many years. I remember when I first joined Delta, I enjoyed listening to employees talk about Dave Garrett, a former CEO, and it was as if they knew him personally. I doubt that very many of them had ever met him. They felt that they had access to him at any time; that if they called his number, he would answer his phone; that if they walked into his office, he would receive them and talk to them. Very few of them took advantage of it, but it was a relationship of trust that existed inside Delta. And you can see that manifest in many ways. People completely trusted the management to take care of them, and I think leadership at Delta also believed that if there was success, everyone would share in it; and if there was failure, everyone would share it. And therefore they were all headed in precisely the same direction. I want to say a little bit more about that as we go on.

But I do think that if you take a look at the airline, what we basically sell are two things: attitude and ability. Our ability, with all the functions we perform, is second to none. The attitude is the crucial difference. Just think of an airplane taking off with 300 people—that flight crew, the hundreds of lives, and very valuable resources that have been entrusted to them. So there is a huge element of trust. Their attitude is crucial, not only because we are a servicing industry where the way people are treated is essential, but also because in the event anything happens those people have to know that the crew are going to handle it in the appropriate and proper way and that they're calling the shots.

And attitude becomes really important when you think about the fact that you've probably had late flights that have been good flights and on-time flights that have been lousy ones. The way our people handle you is fundamental to trust.

But is the leadership of the company on the same wavelength as the employees of the company? I'm going to talk somewhat candidly about this. We've had some difficult times in that respect, as you have seen in the press, and it has affected the company.

So let me take one example. You are sitting on the Board of Directors of Delta Air Lines and you are told that the industry, post-9/11, is in a temporary swoon. It should reverse itself in time, and the normal business performance will come back. In the meantime, we have a team of executives who are essential to the performance of the airline. If they leave the company, what are you going to do? Is it possible we will not be able to run the company effectively or efficiently—or even survive? And because they have plenty of options with other companies wooing them, what are you going to do to keep them?

So someone suggests that you adopt a program that secures their retirement and provides them with compensation incentives to stay with the company through this down period. I must say when that choice is presented to you, you've got to think long, hard, and carefully about it.

At the same time it has to be examined from another point of view, because while your executives are secured, some of your people on the front line are not secured and they are being asked to make sacrifices in terms of working harder and giving up some of the benefits they have expected, including their own retirements and pensions.

And so if you go about securing the executives, you run the risk of alienating the people that work on the line. That was the choice Delta faced in 2002 in the immediate aftermath of 9/11. I need not tell you how that played out. When it was disclosed that the executive retirements had been secured, the rest of the employees came to the conclusion that only the executives were benefiting from the sacrifices everyone was making. And it broke the trust that had always existed inside Delta, which was that we will share victories and we will share defeats and we will share sacrifices as well as gains.

As recently as Friday, I had that question come up while speaking to a group at the company. It is still boiling below the surface. Well over two years have passed. None of the executives here in the company today have those same benefits. All of them are there because it is their passion and their feeling that they want to stay with it and do the right job. And all of them are trying to restore that relationship of trust that we always talk about, that we know is essential in the environment. But we know there is this burning underneath.

All I'm saying is that that trust is a very fragile thing. Once broken, once changed, it's very hard to recover and it's not something that can be done immediately or by just saying the right words. It is built by demonstrated behavior over a long period of time. And interestingly enough, as I talk to my colleagues in the industry, there's also a hangover of lost trust from the actions of Enron, WorldCom, Fannie Mae, and Tyco. People suspect that somewhere, someplace there is a huge stash of dough—and the executives know where it is but they aren't telling anybody else, and somehow they're going to draw on that and take care of themselves and leave the employees on the front line without a grain.

Nothing can be further from the truth in our industry; but nonetheless, there is an element that believes that and as I talk to my colleagues in the airline business they all run into exactly the same thing.

That's one element of the trust relationship. If you're going to lead a company, any company, you have to regain that trust. Simply because you have to say to the people, "Follow me and I'm going to treat you fairly and not take advantage of this for myself." Yet you cannot say that believably if they do not trust you. So trust is absolutely crucial to leading a company like Delta.

There is another piece of the relationship with our passengers besides safety. It has to do with what we call "simpler fares." We were getting enormous pressure from passengers and potential passengers on our fares. We were getting a real push back. In Cincinnati, where fares were among the highest in the country, people were driving to Dayton and to Louisville and to Lexington, Kentucky, to avoid having to pay the fares out of Cincinnati. There were some anomalies that became very difficult to explain. One of those was that a ticket from Cincinnati to New

York cost more than a ticket from Dayton to Cincinnati to New York. When the passengers started thinking about that, they thought something was rotten at Delta. And that's just one example.

As a result of all this, our employees in Cincinnati were getting such pressure that they couldn't wear Delta t-shirts to the supermarket. They were embarrassed about it. When I went to speak to a pilot forum in Cincinnati, I found that the pilots, much to my surprise, were hyped up about how high the fares were because it was embarrassing to them.

So our head of marketing proposed "simpler fares," which simply meant a capped fare so that you knew what the maximum fare was going to be. If the maximum fare was $499 coach and $599 business, this was as much as a 50 percent reduction in previous fare levels. The reaction in Cincinnati was absolutely remarkable. There were two wings in the parking garage of the Cincinnati airport that never had a car in them. They are now filled because we pulled passengers who had been driving to other airports.

People came to trust us, and the best example of that was a very dramatic increase of the number of people willing to use Delta.com, which is our least expensive method of distribution. If you take a company like Southwest Airlines that has a huge patronage on their Web site, people will even use it when they are charging a higher fare because they trust them. I remember reading about a company called Costco, which sold the highest quality at the lowest possible price, and realized we were not giving it to our customers. And in addition, we required a Saturday night stay in order to qualify for the lower fares, which would irritate people. Some businesspeople had to pay it, but if they could get away from it they were going to go to another carrier. It was just one of a whole series of elements that broke trust between the company and our passengers.

If I had to put my finger on one thing that really drove us to adopt simpler fares, it was the desire to regain the long-term relationship with our passengers and potential passengers. To restore that element of trust with them. So again, as in *The Aspect of Love*, this is yet another relationship where trust is fundamental. I'm not going to belabor this topic other than to say that I think that as a company we are extremely conscious of the need for trust in a world where people have lots of choices. They can go with a variety of different selections; so if we are going to be a retail business and draw people in to use our services, they are going to have to trust us. Yes, they are going to want quality. They're going to want comfort and service and so on. But they have to trust that they are going to have it flight in and flight out.

Let me just explain one other element of this. When we started simpler fares and then spread it throughout the system because it worked, we were really becoming a volume-driven airline. It changed the nature of the airline. So we introduced a method of operating the hubs differently. That involved adopting a more continuous flow, rather than having those pulsing peaks about twelve times a day where everything came in all at once and then everything had to depart all at once. During those times, jetways were jammed, gate access was hard to come by, and if you got in early you'd sit out on the runway waiting for a gate to open. It was kind of a bad dream for everyone from baggage handlers to gate agents to flight crews to passengers, especially if you had to get from gates "T" to "E" to make a connection.

So we decided to go to, what we call, "operation clockwork." It has made us a far more reliable company in terms of on-time performance. Our arrival times are better. Our utilization of equipment is better. And, in fact, this has been the equivalent of getting nineteen new aircraft because we are just turning planes faster and getting greater utilization out of our aircraft in the least expensive way. But it was again, part of the trust that we felt we had to have with passengers. If you are going to fly in greater volume, we've got to run a more precise airline.

I want to talk about just one more thing. We are changing a lot about Delta and some of it very fundamentally questions the relationships that existed in the past. I want to talk about one piece of that: outsourcing. Delta has for years, from its very inception, done its own heavy maintenance. Every four, five, or six years, an aircraft is brought in and virtually taken apart and examined, parts replaced as necessary and then reassembled and rolled out. This takes an extensive period of time, is very, very labor intensive, and it's extremely costly. All our competition, both at the network level and at the low-cost carrier level, already outsource that maintenance function.

So we had to face the question: Can we provide the same quality, the same level of safety, the same high performance by continuing to do it in shop, or should we outsource it? And the answer was when you looked at the safety record and talked to the FAA and examined other airlines, you could accomplish all of that while outsourcing the work. But this was not an easy decision to make. It was seen by a lot of people inside Delta as a total break from the past. But nonetheless, it may be necessary if you're going to be competitive, if you're going to get your costs down.

Let me give you an example of what I mean. Virtually every seat on AirTran that takes off in Atlanta is about 65 percent less expensive than every Delta seat. You compensate for that to a certain extent, such as by using a larger aircraft, but you can't compensate for it completely. So we have to get our costs down and we have a limited amount of time to do that. You will see that every major carrier in the country is going to outsource more and more. We chose to outsource to suppliers in North America, while other airlines go to San Salvador, Southeast Asia, and so on. But our choice was to stay in North America where we could, much more readily, supervise the work and make sure it was at our level of quality. But nonetheless, that is the kind of decision that has an effect on trust, because people are going to say to themselves, "If it happens there, am I next?"

My job is to stabilize that feeling and reassure them that this was a decision that everyone agreed to, including the people that are affected by it. We are doing everything we can to cushion that blow.

In closing, let me say one more thing about leadership and trust. When you pick up a newspaper and see that the CEO of X Company made $38 million in a total compensation package, or that another executive made some huge amount, there is a growing feeling that the separation between the management level and the working level is to the disadvantage of employees. It seems to me it would be very hard to lead a company like that. And I don't think I could. But that is the direction things are going and it creates a very difficult problem for the airline industry in its current condition.

It's true that our executives all have other employment options, and we're running a very high risk of losing executives that are extremely valuable. But that concern doesn't completely address the issue. And it could not pardon having a vast separation between the CEO and the rest of the people.

When I took this position at Delta, I strongly felt that I could not lead the company or retain the trust of the people if I was the highest paid person inside Delta, or if I got any kind of bonus or other reward. So, as a result I thought it was personally important to take a very substantial salary cut.[1]

It is, finally, a matter of trust. If they think you're feathering your nest, it is impossible to guide a company in the direction you want it to go.

Well I have, in a self-conscious way, talked about Delta and talked about trust. I thank you for your time and attention.

NOTE

1. Since the time of this speech, Delta entered into a Chapter 11 bankruptcy proceeding. Under Mr. Grinstein's leadership, senior management took additional pay and benefit cuts to further align themselves with frontline employees. At the time of publication of this book, Delta was scheduled to emerge from bankruptcy in 2007. Consistent with Mr. Grinstein's emphasis on re-establishing trust with employees who have suffered significant pay cuts, Delta has proposed that until frontline employees' base pay is restored to industry standard levels, there will not be across-the-board base pay adjustments for senior management. A key component of management's equity based compensation will not pay out unless broad-based employee profit-sharing programs pay out.

CHAPTER ELEVEN

Delivering on Diversity Leadership: A Walk in the Other Guy's Shoes

Cal Darden
Senior Vice President for U.S. Operations, United Parcel Service
February 25, 2003

> Sometimes the easiest and safest way when you're slammed with work is to go by the book. Instead, he looked at the whole picture.

You'll find I'm an eager and open-minded student of diversity management. And a big reason is the nature of my job. I'm an operations guy who happens to oversee a national organization of 320,000[1] employees. They represent a wide range of ages—from college students to retirees—and they run the gamut of ethnic, educational, socioeconomic, and religious backgrounds.

Many of these employees have come to UPS like I did thirty-two years ago—starting at the bottom, working on the loading dock in Buffalo, New York, while pursuing a degree at Canisius College. Like I did then, many today see a career opportunity in the promote-from-within UPS culture.

And like I did then, many today also relish the special deadline challenges of delivering 13 million[2] packages each business day to keep the flow of commerce moving in America and around the globe. I should also note—at last count—the flow of commerce running through the UPS network every day represents about 6 percent of the nation's Gross Domestic Product.

The transportation industry can get into your blood. And it got to me early in my career. You may find it hard to believe, but in my Buffalo days, I used to practice parking and maneuvering eighteen-wheelers in the company parking lot in my spare time. I know that's a little over the top, and I probably should have been spending more of that time studying, but transportation has always been a fascinating business to me. And it still is. It's always evolving, always incorporating new technologies. There's never a dull moment.

Now, as I'm sure you're wondering, how does diversity tie in with such a business? For one thing, few, if any, enterprises require such a large number of employees—individuals representing so many different backgrounds and communities—to come together to work as a *single* team.

Our managers or supervisors must be prepared to jump on a package car when a driver catches the flu, pitch in at the sorting centers during our peak holiday season, or do whatever it takes to keep that flow of packages moving to their destinations. There's no option to put things off until tomorrow. In a nutshell, UPSers are a breed that succeed and advance in their careers through a dedication to meeting deadlines.

And as you might imagine, that requires an organization that must follow rules and procedures. We're famous for our efficiency. And we're proud of it. But we also realize flexibility in a complex world is a necessity too. And, as you'll soon see, instilling a flexible mindset is a key objective of our diversity leadership efforts.

In fact, if the truth be told, we're not all that comfortable with the word diversity. That's because we're more about identifying what people have in common than thinking of how they're different.

And we know if we find that common ground, if we treat all employees with fairness, dignity, and respect, we nurture that high level of teamwork required to meet our demanding deadline challenges.

So diversity—for want of a better word—may not show up as a line item on our balance sheet. But we realize doing it right can add value in a big way. That's why I believe that in well managed, enduring organizations, diversity leadership leads to competitive market leadership.

Within an organization, it can develop business leaders who inspire loyalty and the best efforts of their employees. And externally, diversity leadership can attract investors, as the momentum toward investing in socially responsible companies continues to build.

These are two priorities I want to focus on today. They're significant now. But they're going to be even more compelling in the years ahead as we become an ever more diverse society.

According to the U.S. Department of Labor, in two years 27 percent of the national workforce will be members of minority groups, 48 percent women, and only 38 percent Caucasian. UPS is already ahead of that curve as 35 percent of our total, $360,000^3$-member workforce is now made up of members of minority groups. And 52 percent of our new hires are members of minority groups.

Just last month, the census bureau reported that Hispanics now make up the largest minority group in America. And by the year 2010, nearly one of every six Americans between the ages of eighteen and twenty-one will be Hispanic. And by 2040, half of all Americans will be what we now call "minorities." At the same time, the largest generation of American workers, the 76-million-strong baby boomer generation will be retiring. That will mean the number of jobs requiring digital age skills will greatly *exceed* the number of skilled workers entering the workforce.

So if we do the math, our organizations will be competing to attract and retain employees from a smaller and far more diverse talent pool. As difficult as it might be to imagine now, as the economy recovers, *employees* will replace *employers* in the workplace driver's seat.

What are we doing to be ready for that at UPS? One of the most important ways is by reaching the people in our organization who have the most influence in how employees are treated—our high-potential managers. In fact, we've been at this for thirty-five[4] years through the UPS Community Internship Program, long before anyone even began using the word diversity.

CIP is a sort of "Outward Bound" for diversity awareness. The mind is opened through personal experiences in an environment outside what is familiar. As I said, it's a selective program. Only fifty managers are asked to participate each year. These people are considered to be top performers in mid-level management positions with high advancement potential. They often lead a large number of employees in our district and package sorting hub operations.

While it's considered a vote of confidence to be selected as a CIP intern, the road trip that follows is anything but a boondoggle. The interns leave their jobs behind for one month and travel to a distant community. Last year's interns were assigned to one of these three[5] locations:

• The Henry Street Settlement, a social services agency on the Lower East Side of New York.
• The immigrant border town of McAllen, Texas.
• An Appalachian mountain community near Chattanooga, Tennessee.

They are communities afflicted with poverty, homelessness, spousal abuse, drugs, crime, and gang warfare. We chose an urban location and two rural communities, so that we can assign the managers to an unfamiliar environment. For example, if they have urban backgrounds, we try to assign them to the rural communities. If they're from rural areas, we send them to New York.

Once there, the interns live and eat on-site in accommodations you could only describe as Spartan—just the basics, and close to the areas where they work. The interns immerse themselves in community projects day and night for the entire month. Those projects can involve tutoring preschool Head Start children, orphans, or kids who have AIDS. They may teach resume skills to prisoners or at-risk teens, visit nursing homes and mental health facilities, work in soup kitchens, attach an outdoor shower onto a home, or sometimes just tackle the crisis of the moment.

As you can imagine, the interns are often initially shocked by the challenging living conditions. But after a time, many report seeing the hopefulness of people trying to cope. And the interns see how they can influence that hope.

Imagine, for example, Hispanic women in McAllen, who have never seen a woman in a position of authority, observing a UPS woman organizing a working team. "La Jefa," which means the boss in English, is how those Hispanic women proudly referred to their UPS benefactor. Of course, "La Hefa" (as it is pronounced) took some good-natured ribbing from her fellow male interns. But to her admirers, the phrase was delivered with much respect and admiration.

Throughout their month of service, the interns are required to keep a daily log of activities performed. They also discuss their experiences among themselves and with social workers.

To our knowledge, this is a one-of-a-kind program. Of course, when UPS launched it back in 1968, we weren't anticipating the interdependent world of the twenty-first century. Yet, the company did realize that the civil rights era would usher in a new relationship between the races. And in the late 1960s, UPS leaders were predominantly white men.

Today, more than 1,200 UPS managers[6]—including yours truly—have been through the program at a cost of about $10,000 per intern, or some $13 million since the program began.

We think that investment has yielded a substantial return and here's why. The interns return to work—if not changed people—people with changed perspectives. They're more aware of conditions that exist in our society. They have a better understanding of why those conditions exist. They're sensitive to the reality that problems like homelessness, spousal abuse, and drugs can happen in their back-yard and affect their employees. And on the positive side, they see that hope exists even in the most challenging of environments.

When they return to work, the interns tend to look at employee matters in a less rigid way. They tend to listen with more empathy. Maybe, for example, a single parent is struggling with a sick child, or a car that isn't functioning. Maybe a CIP intern who has worked with disabled kids can better appreciate the demands of an employee with a physically disabled relative. Or, maybe interns will work to bring university-level classes to their work sites to help time and transportation challenged employees. Listening becomes the first step to understanding and improved employee relations.

In addition, the CIP interns often pass along their diversity lessons learned to other managers. They encourage a flexible mindset throughout supervisory levels. And CIP interns have a history of getting involved in their communities by organizing volunteer efforts within their own work groups. This is key since UPS is a decentralized company. We depend on our region and district leaders to be the eyes, ears, and citizen leaders in their communities.

And although there's no way to assign a business value to improved community relationships, we all know that minority buying power is growing. According to the University of Georgia's Selig Center for Economic Growth, minority group buying power has doubled since 1990 to nearly $1.3 trillion in disposable income. And it's expected to reach $2 trillion by 2015.

I know in my own case—although it's been twenty years since my CIP internship in Chattanooga—I still tap into that CIP memory bank when it comes to making policy decisions and recommendations at the board of director level, and in overseeing the company's U.S. Operations.

You know, it's interesting that one of the things workforce researchers say is so important for achieving loyalty in today's stressed workplace is the *simple* act of listening and opening the lines of communication. It's remarkable how far an experience like CIP, one that places you in the other guy's shoes, can help you see that your *real* job as a leader is helping other employees achieve and succeed.

One of my favorite CIP stories is that of intern Mark Colvard who works in my organization as a manager in California. A short time after his CIP experience, Mark had to decide whether to accommodate a driver who needed time off to help an ailing family member. Under company rules, the driver wasn't eligible for the time off. And Mark knew providing it would become a bone of contention among the other drivers in his group.

Nevertheless, he decided to give the driver the two weeks, take some heat, and retain a valuable employee. Mark said he might well have gone the other way before his CIP internship in McAllen. After all, sometimes the easiest and safest way when you're slammed with work is to go by the book. Instead, he looked at the whole picture.

He balanced the circumstances of the employee's personal situation and work performance, and decided against standard operating procedure. In making that call, he helped UPS retain a good employee. And good employees are not easy to replace.

That's the essence of what CIP brings—nudging leadership decisions that treat people with respect, and that help UPS to build a winning team. And, of course, that leads to benefits with our other key constituents as well.

Diversity leadership, for example, is an important factor in a growing trend within the investment community to support socially responsible companies. As many of you may know, publicly held companies are being asked to disclose their community and diversity initiatives to determine whether they are a socially responsible, sustainable enterprise.

How important is that to investors? A recent Harris Interactive/Calvert Group poll shows that seven of ten investors say they want to invest in mutual funds that select companies that are considered socially responsible. Although the components of what goes into defining social responsibility are yet evolving, it's fair to say that it includes a company's philanthropic, environmental, and workforce initiatives.

Yet another way to look at the linkage between workforce initiatives and shareholder value is to evaluate a company's human capital strategy, of which diversity leadership is a key component. In that regard, the Watson Wyatt 2002 Capital Index Study determined that companies with the best human capital strategies had *three* times greater return to shareholders over five years than companies without such strategies.

So diversity leadership is smart business on many levels.

I'm sure some of you are still wondering if CIP could really be the breakthrough program that really helps us achieve those business objectives. We have only anecdotal evidence to measure the impact. But we believe in it. We've never curtailed funding for it when budgets have gotten tight. One thing is certain; this is a program that reaches beyond an information exchange and touches people on an emotional level.

A trainer, for example, could have given Mark Colvard all the relevant information about the McAllen Texas community and culture in a classroom exercise.

Or, Mark could have downloaded a self-study culture module from the Web, and never left home. But could the information itself have caused Mark to change his decision-making process?

Do we all not need to get out of our comfort zones from time to time, to see things from the inside looking out, to really appreciate what diversity is about? CIP differentiates by getting the student to teach him or herself through *living* the experience. It touches an emotional chord. It unlocks an attic in the mind of well-intentioned people that may only be accessible by taking the time to walk in someone else's shoes. We create that time and opportunity for our people, and they take advantage of it.

NOTES

1. UPS employed 360,000 people in its U.S. domestic operations in 2007.
2. UPS delivered 15 million packages a day in 2007.
3. UPS employed 427,000 people worldwide in 2007.
4. UPS had run the Community Internship Program for thirty-nine years as of 2007, at a total cost of $14 million.
5. By 2007 there were four locations for CIP interns; Cameron House in San Francisco was added in 2004.
6. Through 2006, 1,300 UPS managers had participated in CIP.

CHAPTER TWELVE

Leading with Values

Charles M. Brewer
Principal, Green Street Properties LLC
August 16, 2001

> The one downside of having a company that's so visibly and publicly built around a set of values is that when people feel you've let them down, they really feel you've let them down.

I'm talking about my favorite subject today. And I do not claim at all to be on the cutting edge of knowledge about the subject of values-based leadership, but I am absolutely a true believer and I have some real-world experience in attempting to implement it. So I'm going to share some of my thoughts on that subject, some lessons from the MindSpring experience, and a few thoughts about how I see the values-based approach applying in my new field of real estate.

But first, I want to do something that we always did at the start of Mind-Spring company meetings, and that we're starting to do at Green Street Properties meetings: Read aloud our core value and beliefs.

I have surreptitiously distributed nine pieces of paper, numbered 1 through 9, to members of the audience this morning. So as I indicate I am ready, will the person with each number please read aloud the value written there?

Number 1: We respect the individual, and believe that individuals who are treated with respect and given responsibility respond by giving their best.

This is the primary one, the foundation of our set of core values and beliefs. If you think about it, it says that we're going to try to *let* people do great work; rather than *make* them do great work. I think that's how you get the best results. So it's fair to say it has profound implications.

Number 2: We require complete honesty and integrity in everything we do.

This is the second of the two bedrock values. As I look around at companies that are not great places to work, or aren't great places to be a customer, this is the thing that has gone wrong most of the time.

Number 3: We make commitments with care, and then live up to them. In all things, we do what we say we are going to do.

Make commitments with care, and then live up to them. Do what we say we're going to do. Now this value is really a corollary to Number 2. But I wanted it listed explicitly because it's so aggravating doing business today in a world where people just don't do what they say they're going to do. In my estimate, if someone says they are going to do something and will call you back about it by three o'clock tomorrow, the odds of that happening are about 26.5 percent, which is not too good.

Number 4: Work is an important part of life, and it should be fun. Being a good businessperson does not mean being stuffy and boring.

This one is another sort of reaction against the state of business. Some people have the idea that to be a successful businessperson, you have to be a certain way, act a certain way, dress a certain way, and use the word "impactful" seven times every day. A lot of people aren't like that. And if they work at a company where they feel like they have to be like that, they find they can't be themselves anymore, and it's a big problem. I think this one is probably the value that meant the most to a lot of MindSpring employees, because following it meant that people really could be themselves and not have to try to pretend to be somebody else.

Number 5: We are frugal. We guard and conserve the company's resources with at least the same vigilance that we would use to guard and conserve our own personal resources.

Now this one, I certainly wouldn't claim needs to be on everybody's list. But I think that if you're going to use core values and beliefs, and a values-based management approach, you have to adopt the ones that are right for your organization. Obviously some values are for every business, like honesty. But this isn't necessarily one of those. There are plenty of companies that probably can be successful in a flashy, high-spending way—it's just not my way. I don't like it. So although I'm not saying this is the way all companies should be, it is the way that MindSpring was and the way it is today at Green Street.

Number 6: We insist on giving our best effort in everything we undertake. Furthermore, we see a huge difference between "good mistakes" (best effort, bad result) and "bad mistakes" (sloppiness or lack of effort).

This one means, "Give me your best effort." I just want to emphasize the "good mistake, bad mistake" thing, as I think really is a critical difference. If people just get whacked and punished every time they make a mistake, then guess what? Nobody's ever going to try anything. A good mistake, when you give it your best shot, is one you can actually learn something from. You learn what didn't work and know what to try next time. But a bad mistake is a total waste. You still don't know what would have happened if you actually gave it your best effort.

This value is hard to implement, actually, but I would aspire to huge tolerance and forgiveness for good mistakes and almost none for bad mistakes.

Number 7: Clarity in understanding our mission, our goals, and what we expect from each other is critical to our success.

This is especially critical to success if you're following Number 1, and the individuals in the company have a great deal of autonomy and freedom. You better have a common understanding of where you're trying to end up, or you will have chaos.

Number 8: "We are believers in the Golden Rule. In all our dealings we will strive to be friendly and courteous, as well as fair and compassionate.

This value is really just a reminder that our humanity isn't put on hold when we go to work. In fact, it's just as important there as anywhere else.

Number 9: We feel a sense of urgency on any matters related to our customers. We own problems and we are always responsive. We are customer driven.

I wanted that to be sort of the punctuation mark at the end because of the various constituencies the company serves. If customers really are Number 1, we should recognize that without them there is no business. So this was on there as a reminder of that.

So when we talk about how to implement a values-driven approach, we should understand the importance of articulating the values, just as we have done here in this room. We actually do that at every company meeting.

I have spoken about this topic here before, but it has been a little while. So today I am going to use a question-and-answer format where I ask the questions for a while and then you all get to do it later.

I was looking through some old documents recently. I used to write letters all the time to MindSpring customers, as well as speeches, employee letters, and a lot of other things. So I was sorting through some of these documents over the past couple of days, and it was hard, but fun, for me. I hope it's fun for you too.

So the first question that emerges from that material is, "Why this belief in core values to begin with? How did I get on this track?" The short answer is that I found the status quo in business depressing. This was the only thing I could come up with that seemed like it even had a chance of helping me establish a company that would be different from that status quo. So here's something I wrote about that, from my letter to the MindSpring customers in December of 1999:

Our reason for existing as a company doesn't have much to do with the Internet or technology. It's about trying to create a company that really is different and better. We have been frustrated by the status quo in the world of business, both from a customer point of view and an employee point of view. We think the experience that customers have with most companies is pretty bad. Companies often take customers for granted and don't seem to care about serving them well, and often don't even tell them the truth.

Yet it seems to us that most individuals really want to accomplish something wonderful and meaningful with their work, and they are willing to work hard to make that happen. But somehow the organizations they work for make that difficult or impossible, and that's a real tragedy. So we're trying to create a company where people can do great work that they're proud of, and where we provide our customers with an experience that they find truly remarkable.

Even if you start with dissatisfaction with the status quo, it's not so obvious what to do about it. After all, people don't intentionally create companies that are lousy places to work and provide lousy service. So we think the key to creating a company that is different and better is to focus on values. Everything else about a company will change over time. The market, the people, the products—only the values have a chance to remain constant and make the company different and better in a lasting way.

I think that's true. It's really the only path that has a shot.

So the next question is, "Well, did it work?" Yes. There were thousands of ISP users that started around the same time as MindSpring, and our circumstances weren't any different from most of those. We didn't have proprietary advantages of any kind. But somehow we ended up being vastly more successful than any of them. And I really think the core values and beliefs are why.

I have a snippet or two here from a letter back in 1987 where I wrote,

To a large extent, the core values and beliefs manage our company. That means that managers don't have to. We have always been open and honest with our customers and let them know when something is not right. We have done our best to make it right. This fact by itself has made a remarkable difference to our customers. People are not used to businesses telling them the truth. Many times our customers really appear to find it shocking.

And inside MindSpring, core values and beliefs really do a lot of the managing. It's amazing how often they come up spontaneously in every day discussion of what to do in any given situation. Time after time, it happens. The CV&Bs, as w'll call them, can't always provide the answers, but often they do.

And that was one of the most striking things about the culture that grew up at MindSpring. You found people talking about them all the time. If they were trying to figure out how to deal with an abusive customer that was giving us a hard time at the call center, I guarantee that in that conversation people were specifically citing the core values and beliefs. They were talking about respect, and how we have to respect ourselves as well. And they were talking about our duty to serve the customer. And that discussion would help them figure out what to do in that situation.

The next question is, "Is there a key ingredient that you need to make this core value and belief approach work?" And there is. It's authenticity. In fact, I think if you have that, you're almost guaranteed to succeed.

For me, the core values and beliefs really were the whole point of the business, which was to change the way the world does business. I didn't really care if MindSpring was an Internet service provider or a cheese manufacturer. I really didn't. It was how we treated each other, how we treated the customers. So, we just couldn't have been more authentic as far as I was concerned.

Let me share a couple of other quotes here from a book called *Beyond Entrepreneurship*, which was very influential for me in 1991 and introduced me to this concept of the core value and belief approach. I got it out yesterday, and in my memory the whole book was about core values and beliefs. But there are actually just two pages in there about core values and beliefs. Yet somehow they expanded in my mind.

In one part, it explained that the proper question isn't, "What values and beliefs should we have?" Rather, it is, "What values and beliefs do we actually hold in our gut?" It also showed that core values and beliefs get instilled by what you do—by specific concrete actions—not by what you say. And I think that's really true. If the core values and beliefs aren't authentic for the leaders of the company, not only will they fail to influence actions, they will be horribly counterproductive.

The phrase I have used, which is perhaps more colorful than I should employ here, is that people have incredibly accurate BS meters, especially if they get a chance to employ them over an extended period of time. If it's not real, everybody is going to know it's not real. So, there's no point in trying to adopt a set of values that aren't really authentic. You would be doomed to a horrible failure.

And one more note on that: There were a few moments that were critical in forming the great reputation we had with our customers at MindSpring. These were times when something was going wrong, when the values behind us got to shine through so customers could see them.

I discovered one of those, in a letter to customers from November of 1994, when we had just 300 or 400 customers. It said we would be giving all customers a credit of 25 percent of their November fees and acknowledged, "We are not pleased with the service we provided this month." Losing lines at our old site, we had to move the whole network that month. The disruption of the move caused some unexpected busy signals and other problems. I ended with, "Please accept our apologies."

You know, that was sort of a controversial thing to do. We had no money. The company was profitable earlier because there weren't any employees until a couple of months before, but it wasn't profitable at this time. No one had invested in the company but me.

But you know what? We did provide lousy service that month, and this was the right thing to do. It probably cost us a grand total of few hundred bucks, and yet I still hear about that one act today. People remember stuff like that.

So, with authenticity being the required ingredient, the next question is, "How do you implement this core value and belief approach? What actions will you take?" Well, I believe three things are required: (1) you have to articulate the values well and often; (2) you have to select the right people; and (3) you have to look for ways to build the values that will shape the actual structure of the company.

On the articulating side, I'll bet I never once gave any significant address to MindSpring employees where the core values and beliefs weren't a primary theme. I found in a letter to my counterpart at EarthLink as we were discussing merging, he had asked how we did this. My response was,

You want to know how these values make their way of the daily life of the company? Well, here are some of the ways: We start our employee meetings with a recitation. We recite the CV&Bs at the beginning of our annual shareholder meetings. We print them on the back of our business cards. We post them on the website. We discuss them with our customers. We discuss them with our vendors.

In fact, one extra way we did it was in song. So this morning I'm going to sing you a portion of one of the several MindSpring songs. I normally would accompany this with guitar playing, and I made up several songs at different important moments along the way. This was one from January of 1998, when we announced that we were profitable for the first time as a public company. This had been the big strategic goal.

Now to properly interpret this song, you need to know that we started the company with eight zoom modems that I bought from Best Buy. You need to know that we had a three-legged Rottweiler or two hanging around most of the time. And you need to know that after we took over the Harrisburg Hall Center facility from PSI, one of the guys up there got sued based on actions from back in the PSI days. That's probably all you need to know to get the gist of the song.

I used to really worry about these songs. I'd practice them a lot so I could perform them well. But then eventually I came to realize that the worse I was, the better everyone liked it. That really took the pressure off!

This song is to the tune of "Willie," by Little Feat:

Eight zoom modems, a 3-legged dog, a bit of philosophy tacked to the wall. Profit.
Big bad competitors came after us fast, but don't you know that we kicked their_ _ _. Profit.
Then we go from Tucson to Tallahassee, Bakersfield to Buffalo, all the analysts said that
    profit couldn't be made. I guess they had to say something or they wouldn't get paid.
And we did it one call at a time. And we counted our dimes. And we got profit. Bottom
    line profit.

I won't do the second verse. But you know, people would remember stuff like that. They would know that profitability was an important goal.

The second thing you need to do is select the right people. Now that means both at hiring time and also at promotion time. And here is a little nugget from back in 1997. It says the core and values beliefs had made hiring easy.

We've grown from 0–380 employees in 3 years. We have never paid a recruiting fee, and we have never paid for an advertisement. Most people who hear about our core values and beliefs thing think, "Oh, that's interesting." But that's it. Some people think, "Right. Sounds good, but these people are horribly naïve. They are going to get crushed out in the real world." But there are some people who hear about what we're trying to be and they say, "Wow, I've been looking for a company like that my whole life. I have to work at MindSpring." So those people are the ones we hire.

Luckily for us there were enough people that fell in that category and were turned on by what we were trying to do that they just came to us. It really was an incredible advantage.

But it's not just hiring the right people, it's also about who gets ahead. And if the people who end up ascending to the senior leadership positions aren't ones who are the best exemplars and role models for the core values and beliefs, you're going to have an authenticity question. So that is super-critically important.

Now, what are the difficulties of this value-based approach? There's really only one that I come up with. And its what might be called "leading with your chin." The one downside of having a company that's so visibly and publicly built around a set of values is that when people feel you've let them down, they *really* feel you've let them down. And this applies to both customers and employees. There are times when people, even reasonable ones, violently disagree on what the proper applications of these values are in any given situation. And when that does happen, it can lead to very strong, emotional reactions. People feel truly betrayed.

For example, I once got six e-mails in two days from one customer who felt we had lied to him and deceived him because we were discontinuing the use of a server product that let our customers post a particular type of audio file on their personal Web pages. He specifically, and in detail, described how this action violated six of our nine core values and beliefs. In my opinion, we violated none, and his position was really all but absurd. But I assure you it was strongly held. He even said that the reason why he was so upset with us was because he had thought that we were really different. And he closed his e-mail with the statement, "Hell hath no fury like a customer scorned."

So, that's the only real difficulty that I could come up with. If you follow this approach, you're going to be setting expectations high. So if you don't follow through, or even if people reasonably disagree and think you're not following through when you think you are, it can stir some real emotions.

Are there any other dangers to be aware of in this approach? Well, I think success itself can endanger the core value and belief approach. It's not exactly a danger of employing the values, but a difficulty that you might encounter as you have success. And I had something else to say about that in a customer letter. This is August of 1998:

Those of you who have been around us for a while, know that MindSpring's whole reason for being has to do with being a different and better kind of company based on respect for the individual, honesty and integrity. Our appeal has always been built around things like, telling the truth, trying hard, doing the right thing when you get the chance, and behaving like caring human beings. I sort of think of us as the Forest Gump of the Internet.

On the other hand, you also know that MindSpring has come a long way in a short time. With 627 employees and 393,000 customers, we're not so small anymore. You might be wondering how our original ideas are holding up. Well, I'll be the first to tell you that success is not without its perils. I personally feel like the world has formed a conspiracy to turn me into a conceited jerk. My alma maters, which in the past regarded me as deviant and potentially unsavory sort of graduate, are claiming me with pride. TV shows invite me to make appearances. Newspapers and magazines print articles about MindSpring. I get invited to make speeches—often on topics I know nothing about. And worst of all, guys I played basketball with for years all of a sudden don't foul me anymore.

One possible explanation for all this that in the last couple of years, I've suddenly become much more charming, witty, intelligent, handsome, and athletic. Unfortunately, there are eyewitnesses who can provide beautiful testimony that no such transformation had taken place.... To some extent, everyone here at MindSpring is tempted by these same devils. Granted, when most of our employees go up for a lay-up, they still get hammered. But, we're no longer the underdogs we used to be. We used to be those poor fools working in an industry where all the experts said no one can ever make any money. Our death was always predicted to be eminent.

Now we seem to be the toast of the town. We win "best buy" awards from leading national publications. We're making money, the stock price is soaring and success brings the temptation of complacency. Temptation to forget about all the little things that got us here in the first place. Temptation to simply assume that we are better than our competitors rather than really working to make it so.

Our antidote for this temptation is to constantly go back to the core values and beliefs that helped us get here in the first place.... There's nothing we have created here at MindSpring that cannot be destroyed very quickly by a small dose of arrogance.

You know what, I think we did suffer. I think some doses of that arrogance did creep in, and it was a bit of a battle for us.

Next question: "Does it scale? Can this work in a big company?" I say it scales to infinity. In fact it scales incredibly well, but it requires that everybody in the company become a champion and guardian of the core values and beliefs. And if only one person is in that role, say the founder, I think it can scale to about three people, and that's about it. So it takes everybody for it to scale beautifully, especially those in some of the tougher, grinding kinds of jobs, like the sales desk where people are answering the phone and dealing with the same very limited range of questions time and time again.

The new people coming in really had a tendency to help everybody else get fired back up again. Because after slogging away for a while, it is easy to forget some of the good things about MindSping and about that job. There had been people who would come in from less-desirable environments and be wildly enthusiastic with what they found. And that would remind the rest of us that we did have something that was special.

Another frequent question is, "How does the values-based approach apply when making acquisitions?" We did a lot of acquisitions, and we learned that if you're going to stand for something, you cannot stand for everything. If you're going to be a great place for some people to work, you can't be a great place for all people to work. People who don't fit need to be ejected, and you just need to realize that in an acquisition the people who work in the company you are acquiring didn't choose you, they didn't choose your core values and beliefs, and some of them just won't embrace those values. Those people have to go, and they have to go fast.

But with that done, I think acquisitions can work out great for a values-driven company. In fact, my single favorite moment in all of MindSpring history was when we did our first acquisition and we bought a customer-base that took us from being regional to national. And in the process we took over a facility up in Harrisburg, Pennsylvania, where they had close to as many employees as we had in Atlanta. It had been a hell hole. The people they were providing horrible customer support and they hated the company, everything was upside down about the metrics and how that place ran, and so we came in.

We sent Chris Miller up there, one guy from Atlanta, to kind of be ambassador. It was the same people and same facility, but within just a couple of weeks, the service they were providing was great. In fact, a little while after that they were kicking Atlanta's butt in quality and quantity! You know what happened? I'd say it was like we were the liberating army, showing up with sincere dedication to a philosophy that was appealing. You know, we were the Americans showing up in Paris and it was fabulous.

Next question: "Does the core value and belief approach apply in a merger?" That's a little bit tougher one. In a true merger of equal situations, or anything that's even close to that I think, it's a lot less predictable what the culture and values of the new company will turn out to be. And in the case of the MindSpring/ Earthlink merger, I really don't know how it's turning out now. And even if I did, it's not my place to comment about it. But I do know that during the time I was there, it was a big struggle.

And I'm not saying anything bad about the Earthlink people. They just hadn't grown up with this same set of values and the same philosophy of making the values the bedrock of the company.

So another question is, "What about the conflict with profit maximization and duty to shareholders in a public company?" There is no conflict here, but outsiders often imagined there was one. So this is a question that I've faced many, many times. I wrote about it in a customer letter in May of 1996, right after we went public. It said, "There is absolutely nothing inconsistent between driven by our core values and beliefs and working to maximize shareholder value. If fact, we believe that dedication of the core values and beliefs is what drives shareholder value." And that's really the nut of it; I still would certainly agree with that.

So, "Will the same values-based approach work in your new arena of real estate?" Well, what's different in this business is that most of the people that will be responsible for helping us deliver an exceptional product or service won't actually be employees of our company. So, I do think it's going to be harder, or at least different. We're not going to have the capability of selecting all the individual people that are involved. We're not going to have the chance to be in front of them articulating the values as frequently. But we're going to try, and I suspect there are going to be some interesting lessons and challenges that come out of it.

And finally, "So why the heck are you going into real estate?" It's a good question. The reason is that I have a very strong passion for the product that I'm hoping we will produce. And at MindSpring, as I said, that wasn't necessarily the case. We could just as easily have been a cheese manufacturer. But this time I really have a passion for the line of business as well as the values.

Whether your concern is about environmental problems or social problems, I think this whole question of land use and how we create our built environment is just looking for solutions. I think the conventional suburban development patterns we've been practicing for the last fifty years is pretty much an environmental disaster and have caused a lot of social problems also. And on top of that, I just personally find it very, very unappealing.

So, do I think the principles to follow to create something better are clear? I think we can create a built environment that will be much better for the natural world and also much better for our social well-being. And I think it will be much more appealing to a lot of people, including me. So I want to help create that, and that's why I've chosen this particular line of business.

One closing note. I want to share with you one particularly moving e-mail that I got from a real talented young MindSpring employee, shortly after I left Earthlink. I think this is proof positive that a values-based approach to leadership in business really can make a big difference in people's lives. That's enough motivation to keep me going for a long time. It says,

I'm sure you've received a ton of similar messages but I just wanted to add my personal thanks for all that you've done for me in my career. Your leadership values and the great company you've created were a profound relief from the typical cynicism which afflicts my generation. All my life I've known that I would eventually start my own business. Your example has shown me that I can be a wildly successful entrepreneur while still maintain my values. In fact, I firmly believe that it was those very values which made MindSpring the success that it was. People want to be inspired; they want to feel that they are part of something important. They want to have fun at work, they want to be trusted and challenged and treated like adults; at least the best workers do. And once people have tasted an intelligently run organization, they will not or cannot return to business as usual.

You created all of this, Charles. You gave this opportunity to literally hundreds of people if just a few of us take these lessons and spread them to new businesses, then maybe we can still change the way the world does business. Thank you for inspiring me to not accept the status quo and to demand more from my employment than a paycheck and medical benefits. Thanks.

NOTE

Charles Brewer was founder, chairman, and CEO of MindSpring Enterprises until its merger with EarthLink Network to form the second largest Internet service provider. In 2001 he launched a new venture, Green Street Properties, a development firm specializing in "new urbanism" and smart growth.

CHAPTER THIRTEEN

Have You Hugged a Teamster Lately?

Robert J. Rutland
Chairman, Allied Holdings Inc.
April 14, 2000

> The challenge with a union workforce is that the process of getting to a
> labor contract is very contentious, so there are often a lot of hard and
> harsh feelings that have a tendency to last for many, many years.

Have you hugged a Teamster lately? This was a question we frequently asked
ourselves in the last negotiations of our master contract with the Teamsters union.
The intent of it was to emphasize that we have a good relationship with our Teamster workforce, contrary to the popular perception of the unionized workforce,
especially the Teamsters.

Our company has been in business for sixty-five years at this point and we have
seen a lot of change as the automobile business has evolved, and as transportation itself has evolved. We began in 1934, and after a pretty significant beginning
we experienced the difficulties of World War II, which closed down the automobile industry and converted our trucks to hauling troops for the war. After the
war we reclaimed our trucks and put them back into automobile transportation
service.

Then in the late 1950s, rail entered the automobile transportation business,
adding another dimension as we became interlined with rail at manufacturing
facilities all over the country.

In the late 1970s, we went through deregulation, which meant we no longer
had a franchise for our part of the country—and also that anyone anywhere in the
country could take advantage of transportation into our area.

By the early 1990s, we decided to go public to allow our business to take
advantage of deregulation for expansion.

Along with all this growth came a lot of internal change. We are familiar with
change. And looking at our history we realize that one of the most significant
early changes, outside of World War II, occurred in the early 1950s when our
company entered into an organized labor agreement. This was primarily because

the automobile manufacturers' workforces were unionized and they wanted us to be unionized as well when we went onto their facilities.

The challenge with a union workforce is that the process of getting to a labor contract is very contentious, so there are often a lot of hard and harsh feelings that have a tendency to last for many, many years. In fact, we even experienced some dynamiting of our trucks and other very hostile acts during that period.

The perception of organized labor, for those of you who are not close to it, is that they are in a hate/love relationship with the company. So we, as a company that is run by Christian principles, decided early on in the 1960s that if we were going to be successful and give good service and quality to our customers, we needed to be on the same team as our workforce. We developed a very strategic plan to draw our workforce closer to the management of the company and to the customers. We developed a system of core values, which for us meant that we would operate by Christian values. This did not mean that we would evangelize our workforce, but we would manage our workforce with love, care, and hope. These qualities would be a thread that moved through all our stated values and corporate mission.

We also strategically determined that we would have two parallel plans for developing our company as we grew. One was that we would build it on our core value system, and the other was that we intended to be the best in our industry in the way of growth, quality, and profitability. As Jim Collins stated in the book *Built to Last*, case studies have shown that good companies change, but their values never change. Similarly, methods often change but principles never do. This is the foundation we used to build this parallel course for future success.

All of us in the Rutland family—my brother Guy Rutland, III, my dad Guy Rutland, Jr., and myself—felt like we were called to be Christian businessmen and that we could run a business by biblical principles and be very successful, which is probably very contrary to popular belief. Our intent was to bring unity to our workforce and to defuse the hostility. We put up posters around our company to indicate that we wanted our employees to know who we were, not what we were.

As we tried to develop a strategy to run the company by love, care, and hope, we had to be conscious of the type of business we were in, which was a diverse workforce of people who were away from us for most of their working careers. In other words, they were on trucks delivering automobiles to dealers, around the Southeast initially and ultimately all over North America.

So we began to use the term "hugging the Teamsters." We have to be very conscious of the physical, emotional, and social aspects of an organized labor force, which is responsible for contacting our customers and is the ultimate delivery point to automobile dealers on a day-to-day basis. When we made our first step to develop the core values and put in place a strategy to be the best company in our industry, our motto was "The World's Best Car Haulers." We have always strived to have that reputation in our industry. We have always been a leader and the best in service and quality.

As we continued to grow, we had to find a way to extend our value systems into our far-scattered operating territories. So we developed a corporate chaplaincy, which we called a ministry of presence. This placed an individual chaplain in each of our locations, some on a contract basis, others full-time employees, who were there to minister to the needs of our employees, both management as well as the union workforce.

We believed the presence of chaplains in our workplace could help meet the needs of individual families, because it was very clear to all of us that employees do not leave their problems at home, but in fact they bring them to work. We believed it would be a strength if we could be sensitive to our employees and have a way to minister to their needs.

Let me give you one example. We had a driver who had been with us for twenty-five or thirty years, who had a heart attack and died while driving the truck. We made an impression on his son's mind and spirit by having our chaplains present in that crisis and by reaching out to the family, as well as by having people in management reach out to them. In fact, this made such an impression on the son that he later became a chaplain as he grew older and went through his education.

We also use our chaplaincy to reach out to employees at funerals and weddings, during illness, and other crises they may experience. We do not interfere with their relationships with their own places of worship, but statistics have shown that 75 percent of the population in the country is not involved in a church on a regular basis, so many do not have a church family to help minister to them. We want to try to provide that. As you can imagine, in a large workforce there are times when there are stressful situations with the union. We have had strikes, but our chaplains have continued to minister to the people, not taking a position on the issues. The only chaplain I had to release from our employment was one who decided he would take the union position, which alienated him from management and meant that he could no longer have a ministry with them. You have to be very careful in that role. The chaplains do not report to human resources; they report to the chief executive of the organization so that they have confidentiality privileges and are not required to tell what they know about the employees unless it is of some critical nature or safety concern. We think this is a reason we have been able to go through strike situations and continue to work with our workforce and move cars for the customers while honoring the strike requirements.

Another thing we do to reach out to our employees is to host picnics at each of our terminals with senior management representatives participating in each one. This allows everyone to be on the same level in a family-type atmosphere. No alcohol is served and there is no "colorful" behavior, but there are ballgames and dunking booths and the things that allow people to laugh together and fellowship together. This helps employees see that our management are real people and it lets our management see that these people are down to earth and should be respected as individuals.

For many years we also sent *Guideposts* magazine, originated by Dr. Norman Vincent Peale, to the home of each of our employees. This was not done to send any particular message about our faith, but to give them some stories of people who have gone through crises and dealt with them successfully. This little magazine embraces our core value of hope, and we received a lot of good feedback from it because it was not intimidating or threatening, just good everyday stories about peoples' lives.

As I mentioned, enacting the core values was one part of a dual, or parallel, strategy for success. So as we worked on strengthening our relationships with our employees, we also developed a program called Performance Management to try to change the behavior of the workforce to be more in line with our customers' requirements of quality and service. This program was based on strategy of managing more by the carrot than the stick. An expert named Aubrey Daniels, who worked with us to develop this, showed that people's behavior is directly related to the reinforcement they receive. In other words, if misbehavior gets reinforced it will continue. But if reinforcement follows good behavior you tend to get better behavior. Rather than hitting people when they did something wrong, we tried to recognize what they did right and recognized them for it.

You might imagine that a unionized workforce would be suspicious when we started this program, but once they realized we were sincere about it, and saw that it fit the core values of our company, it became very successful. We had more difficulty with our management than our employees, because managers had a tendency to be negative and criticize people for doing things wrong, yet they were not conscious of the right things. Our Performance Management program required that managers provide four positive reinforcements for each negative.

This even had an impact on people's home lives. We had families tell us that it proved to be very effective when our managers used this theory of positive reinforcement, rather than negative, at home.

So what results did all this get? It ultimately improved our turnover in the workforce, which in the trucking industry can be close to 100 percent a year. Through these types of initiatives and applying our core values, we reduced turnover to just 5 percent. We also had a 30 percent increase in productivity and quality.

We rewarded employees with everything from coffee mugs to jackets to hats. We created a "Top Gun" recognition and printed this on caps for our top performers. They wore these with pride when they went into the dealerships and were known for their performance. We had celebration dinners and other awards of recognition. We became the pacesetter for our industry. We saw a lot of our competitors pick up similar types of activities, but none ever achieved our efficiency and level of performance.

And we continued to honor our people in retirement. Since our Company had been in business for sixty-five years, we had a lot of retirees who had gone through their entire working careers as part of the life of the company. So we brought them together at our picnics to interact with our current employees, and they had a tendency to tell them what a good place Allied was to work. This impressed the newer, younger employees. At Christmas and Valentines Day we would get everyone together and feed them and share experiences and good fellowship with retirees, management, and unionized workers.

We made it a point to periodically survey our entire workforce, not just management or supervision, but also our truck drivers, mechanics, and yard people who were in the union. We asked them what they thought about the way we were running our company. We had Gallup come in and develop a simple survey, because as you can imagine, the typical driver will not sit and fill out an hour-long survey questionnaire. We used thirteen questions to ask them things like, "Are we living up to our core values"; "Are we a company of integrity"; "Are we serving the customers the way we say we are?" We would then share this feedback with our workforce to let them know how things were moving. Every time we ran a survey we got high marks on our core value implementation, the way we operated our company, and the integrity level of our management when dealing with the workforce. It gave us benchmarks to move on and a clearer understanding of how our employees saw us and how we might be perceived in the eyes of our customers. It helped us stay focused on running the business by good principles.

All these steps I have described helped us many times as we moved to negotiate with the union. We insisted that our management negotiate and handle their labor relations with the same core values. For that reason we were able to achieve one of the highest levels of success in the industry, for we did not have as many grievances as our competitors or as many discharges. We worked with our workforce and held to our values and principles. This was essential in our labor relations because the representatives of the Teamsters union knew that when we said we would do something, we did it with integrity. When we presented our case in negotiations, we did so honestly, and we did not practice winning at all costs. Our success in labor relations became very vital part of how we operated our company on a day-to-day basis.

As we began to move through deregulation across the United States, we began to acquire other companies, including one that had over 90 percent of the Canadian car-haul business. We brought the same parallel management strategy to each of these companies. In other words, we applied the same core values, we put chaplains in their locations, and we implemented the same standards of performance and supervision. As we moved west and northeast and all across Canada, we saw the same type of improvement in turnover, efficiency, and productivity by managing on a more positive basis.

Along the way we have continued to evaluate our strategy. We are more convinced than ever that it was very wise to adopt the parallel approach many years ago. We have seen that employees are brought into a closer relationship with management and each other when they are treated with integrity and respect. Just as important, we have seen a payoff in achieving the level of efficiency that our customers have come to expect.

So to many of you "Hug a Teamster" may sound like a funny expression, but to us it is a serious commitment. It may not always be a physical hug, but emotionally and socially we send a message that we respect you, that we honor you with integrity, and that you are very much a part of our company. We have found that our employees have reciprocated by hugging us, not only by caring about the company but also about the customers.

I hope some of this has been of interest to those of you who have not experienced a unionized workforce. But whatever your business may be, I will say that if you are looking for a success strategy, it must not be one that is so focused on efficiency and profitability that you forget about the integrity and respect that is due to your employees. A strategy based on sincerely held values can bring unity to your workforce and create a much more friendly and exciting atmosphere to operate a business.

CHAPTER FOURTEEN

Leadership Challenges of Building a Company in Today's Environment

John Wieland
Chairman and Chief Creative Officer of John Wieland Homes and Neighborhoods
February 17, 2004

> One thing I've learned is that when your integrity is challenged, you need to handle that at the top.

I want to share with you seven basic thoughts about our company, John Wieland Homes and Neighborhoods, that I've learned over the past thirty-four years. The first is the critical nature of core values. Back in 1994, I had a life-changing experience when I read this wonderful book that many of you may have read—*Built to Last* by Jim Collins and Jerry Porras. One of the great parts of that book was where they talked about core values and the importance of formalizing those core values. So in 1995, we had sixty people at John Wieland Homes read the book, and they came up with nearly fifty different suggestions for what our core values ought to be. We eventually decided on five core values, and they have really stood the test of time.

First is excellence—we just think that is so fundamental. The second is presentation and is fairly unique to us—how we look, how our homes look, and how our homes look when the customer moves in. The third is passion, and in the homebuilding business you have to have it. Then, the fourth is one I will talk a little more about later—integrity. And the fifth is completeness. We've found out as homebuilders that if we do every little step completely, then when we get to the end we have a successfully completed home. Together, these turned out to spell "epic," and so those became our epic core values. Excellence, Presentation Passion, Integrity, and Completeness. As I said, they have really withstood the test of time.

For the second key, we go to another book by Jim Collins, *Good to Great*. There are wonderful things in this book as well, and one of them is to get the right people on the bus. The corollary to that, of course, is to get the wrong people off the bus. One of the things we do to get the right people is to test extensively. For example, by the time we hire someone they have been through such a gamut of tests that they know they are the right person. We test for integrity, we test for traits, we test for mental processing, and then we have a consulting psychologist. But the thing we have found is that if you have really strong cultural values, then the people who don't fit with those cultural values become what the book calls self-ejecting. And that really does work—the people who decide that they really don't fit voluntarily go elsewhere. Sometimes, of course, it doesn't happen, and you have to provide a little incentive to relocate, but we work very hard to do the right things on that.

Also very important at John Wieland Homes and Neighborhoods is training. We have Wieland University, and it offers eight different curriculums. In fact, we were recognized in 2003 by *Training* Magazine as having the 53rd best training program in the United States—right behind IBM and Cisco. We're very proud of that, and we think our training is really fundamental to how you grow a great business.

The third thing I'd like to mention is to not outgrow your quality. We went through a really bad period with this in the mid-1990s. We were growing very fast—the market was hot and sales were terrific. But there was a real shortage of good subcontractors in Atlanta, and we built some homes that weren't quite as good as they should have been. And then we had a terrible experience—we expanded to Nashville, Tennessee. One of the things that we found out in retrospect was that all the good contractors in Nashville were already busy, so that meant we got all the bad trade contractors. We really paid dearly for that experience.

In homebuilding, it is important to never underestimate how truly unhappy an unhappy homeowner can be. They can be really unhappy, and they can make you unhappy too. We found out that there is a whole infrastructure made up of lawyers and doctors and consultants and inspectors that is designed to assist people who are really unhappy. And they come out and they say things that you know are not the truth, but that they are paid to say. What we learned out of that experience is that it makes a lot sense to get very generous very fast.

Now we have a sort of an assessment process. The first step is to ask if this is an unhappy person. If the answer is yes, then the second question we ask is if this is an unhappy person who can be really nasty. And if that answer is yes, then we just walk right over there and tell them, "We love your home, so why don't you just sell it back to us, and we'll terminate all this discussion." That doesn't happen but maybe once or twice a year; but if you offer to buy back someone's house, they usually get happy. Oftentimes they'll say, "You know, we love the neighborhood, so we'd just like you to get us another new home in this neighborhood." And we'll do that. So in the end, it was a very educational experience being in Nashville—so educational that I'll never forget it. We lost enough money up there to keep us humble, but we did make everybody happy.

The fourth principle is that you have got to massage your bankers. Homebuilding is really all about credit—if there is a loan available, there's going to be a house. And one of the important things we have learned about bankers is that you have got to stay in touch with them. E-mail is important for that—bankers absolutely love e-mail because it lets them know you're still in business. I don't know whether you've heard the story about the builder that called his banker on Monday morning and asked, "Is Mr. Swartzhiemer there?" and the receptionist said, "No, I'm terribly sorry. Mr. Swartzhiemer died over the weekend." And then the builder hung up. About ten minutes later, the phone rings again and the voice says, "Is Mr. Swartzhiemer there?" and the receptionist again says, "No, Mr. Swartzhiemer died over the weekend. But haven't you called before?" The builder then said, "Yes, I just like the sound of your answer."

The fifth key that I'd like to share today is trust—you must trust your people. Hopefully you've selected them well, and hopefully they have adopted your core values. I will personally confess that trusting completely was a very hard thing for me to do. However, if people are going to learn, people are going to make mistakes. I have always admired Mills B. Lane, who was CEO in the late 70s and early 80s of Citizens & Southern Bank, which is now part of Bank of America, because he would call mistakes research and development. You can't get away with doing that anymore in the corporate world, but I think it is a pretty good thought, because mistakes are research and development for your people. Only by learning to step back and let some mistakes happen, and then trusting our people enough to know that they are working very hard and are very talented, have we been able to grow.

The sixth item is what I call growing the brand. It is the idea of focusing on overall value, with price as only a part of the value equation. It is the overall experience of buying a home and owning that home that really makes the difference. Interestingly enough, if you go back and talk to customers after they have moved in, they are going to talk much more about the experience than they are going to talk about the price or one specific characteristic or another. So, part of our strategy is to be customer-centered by creating an overall buying-owning-service experience that is reinforcing for the customer.

We try to be special as a company and make our neighborhoods special. And we focus on longevity—on the fact that we've been in business for thirty-four years, and hopefully we'll be in business for thirty-four more. Lastly, we focus on providing something better to that homeowner because they need a reason to move. Some people thankfully transfer to Atlanta and need a home, and that's a great part of our business. Another really important part of our business is helping people in Atlanta who want to stay in Atlanta find a new home, and we're very proud to offer them a great product.

The seventh and most important item is integrity, and as I mentioned before, that's one of our core values. Interestingly, in the book *Built to Last*, integrity is the core value that appears in almost every company's list of core values. But not everybody takes that value seriously, and that is a great tragedy for American business. Hopefully we'll get past this, but it doesn't look like we are past it quite yet. One thing I've learned is that when your integrity is challenged, you need to handle that at the top. We get a variety of mails on a variety of subjects, and every now and then we get a letter that questions our company's integrity. When Joan

Trimble, my executive assistant for over twenty years, and I spot that letter, we jump right on it. People often don't really mean their complaints—they often are having a bad day and get carried away. When you quickly address their concerns with them, you can often clear up those misunderstandings very quickly.

That is seven items, but I've actually got an eighth. Sharing has always been important to us, and it has always been important to me—important thirty years ago, twenty years ago, and now. One of the projects we're engaged in now is building what we call the Second Mile Home in partnership with our trade contractors. It is an almost ten thousand square foot structure that has eleven apartments in it, and we gave it without any cost to the Atlanta Union Mission for their use as a transitional residence for women and children. We've also built and donated the Wieland Wildlife Home at Zoo Atlanta, and we've built more then two dozen homes for Habitat for Humanity. It has been great to partner with our trade contractors and our suppliers in this way, because so often they are happy to be generous, but nobody asks them to give. So we give them that opportunity. One of the things that I was told a long time ago is that you can't out-give God. I think that is really true.

CHAPTER FIFTEEN

Ethics First: A Reform Agenda for City Government

Shirley Franklin
Mayor of the City of Atlanta
March 27, 2002

> He didn't care who I was, and didn't look up to find out; but I knew that
> it was time for a change if a 10-year-old saw the problem.

It's a pleasure to be with you, and it's a good way to start the morning to be among people who care about Atlanta and love Atlanta. But it is also my pleasure to talk to you about an issue that is really on the hearts and minds of many people throughout the City. During the campaign season it became very clear that the key issues in the campaign were integrity, trust, and honesty. And it became clear to me about a year into the campaign that people would vote for the person they trusted. We could talk about everything—we could have great programs—but in the end, people vote for whom they trust. And if they don't trust any of the candidates, they don't vote, which says a lot about American democracy.

So, I started my administration with an initiative related to ethics—ethics in government. The first requirement was to work with our council members, and I appreciate their willingness to engage in the discussion of ethics. We had to balance the City's budget, as required by the City's Charter and state law, so that was the first thing to do, but the second was to propose some fairly significant changes to the City's ethics code and the way we operate, and to set that standard early.

Throughout the campaign, many of you challenged me and other candidates, who were running for various positions, on the issue of changing how the City operates. How we would change the procurement process. How you would know that it is fair and open and competitive. In fact, Common Cause actually hosted a forum for the three mayoral candidates, specifically focused on ethics. And my proposal then is exactly what I did; I formed an outside task force of people who had a variety of experiences: A retired dentist who had been an elected official in one of the outlying areas who now lives in Atlanta; a former assistant U.S. Attorney; a former college president; and several others who came together to review the City's ethics code and various proposals that had been discussed in the City. I asked them to come up with their best thinking, and my commitment to them was that if they would spend the time, I would introduce—unedited—their proposals to the City Council, and that I would initiate, by administrative order, their proposed changes, until the Council could take formal action.

And this is what they found. They found that the standards of conduct in the current ethics code were inadequate. In particular, the rules regarding outside income and gratuities as conflicts of interest, including financial disclosures, had to be strengthened. They found that the ethics code contained ineffective enforcement mechanisms and that the Ethics Board does not presently have the power necessary to effectively enforce the existing standards. They found that the City must improve employee communications and the training, so that they understand that ethical training is an integral part of the job. And they found that there was no single employee within City government who had the job of monitoring compliance with the City's ethical standards. And to that end, they made several fairly strong recommendations, some of them guided by the work of the Georgia Regional Transportation Authority, to adopt a very stringent code.

They recommended a newly structured and empowered Ethics Board, where four of the five members would be appointed by outside organizations, and the fifth member, would be appointed by the Mayor. And this appointee would be proposed from the recommendations of a fifth outside organization, so that there would be checks and balances throughout the appointment process. They urged that the Ethics Board be independent and empowered to initiate investigations, as opposed to just responding to others' investigations or complaints. They said the Ethics Board should have the power and the responsibility of receiving the disclosure reports of public officials, whether department heads or elected officials.

Now, maybe that last item doesn't seem like a big thing. But there are gross inadequacies in the way financial disclosures are prepared. I discovered that during the campaign and, frankly, there's no one presently who monitors those disclosures. So this change gives the Ethics Board the responsibility of insuring that the disclosure is in keeping with the law and that the disclosures are complete. This is an innovation that came from Judge Dorothy Kirkley, who chaired this committee.

I want to say more about the notion of an ethics officer, one person within city government, operating with very limited support staff, because it would not be necessary, who would assist the Board in their investigations, receive complaints, either on a confidential basis or some other basis, and who would train city employees. So this would be the person within city government who would be known as someone who could answer your questions. Our City Council president indicates that throughout her public career, she has called on the Ethics Board of the State of Georgia for interpretations. This would put such a person in city government.

And our committee recommended that the Board have the power to discipline— to assess the administrative sanctions up to $1,000 per violation, to publicly reprimand, to recommend suspension or termination of employees, and to suspend or debar city contractors for violations. Now there are other aspects of this proposal, but I wanted to share with you that the Ethics Board would now be in a position to assist the City in representation of all of its citizens so that we would not have these recurring rumors associated with violations that go undocumented and uninvestigated throughout years and years and years.

This would be a very strong Ethics Board. And I think that is a good thing. There are other proposed measures in the ordinance that has been proposed to the Council, including a zero tolerance for any conflict of interest. This means that if a company or individual is doing business with the city, or seeking to do business with the city, then city officials, from top to bottom, are prohibited from taking any gratuity or gift of any kind, other than something nominal gift like a plaque or recognition for participation in a program.

If an individual company were sponsoring a table this morning, for example, I would not have been able to eat without paying. (Now my doctor would say that would not be a bad thing, because I could do without a few meals!) This changes the standard of interaction and makes it perfectly clear to both sides when anyone is crossing the line. And our plan allows for you to go to an ethics officer for clarification if there's any question in your mind.

Now a meal doesn't seem like a big thing, but the committee decided that instead of having a threshold like $25, which can get complicated, there should be zero tolerance. In anticipation that the Council—eight new members of the Council, a new Council president—would have very good reasons for public debate of these new ethics initiatives, I issued an administrative order that covers all employees in city government, who are under my direct supervision. This order covers everyone except the Council, Council staff, and the judicial agencies. The rest of us will begin training within the first sixty days for department directors and others.

I am proud of this legislation, not because I designed it, but because it worked to have an outside group come in to set a standard, a very high standard. It allows us to get buy-in from the rest of the community. Those who participated did so because they love Atlanta too, and they want us to avoid the confusion and the rumor mill that we've experienced in the last few years.

In addition to all this, I have set up a tips line that city employees can call on a confidential basis, either to report violations or suspected violations, or to ask questions. And I have appointed an interim ethics officer, one of our deputy city attorneys. And ask the city attorney every week whether we are getting calls, and he assures me that we are and that people care—employees care. We also introduced an intranet in city government last week, which allows employees to access the administrative order and other policies on line, so that helps to educate the employee population and the workforce.

There will be a lot of discussion at the Council in an effort to be sure this is a policy they can support. I would expect that in the next thirty to forty-five days the Council will pass nearly all of what has been proposed. And I'm not quibbling about that. I think that there is a role for the legislative body to consider this over a period of time. But I expect that they will find, in the end, that this is the work of some very fine minds and that it will set Atlanta apart, not just in the State of Georgia, but also across the country. That it is certainly within our reach.

Some of you have heard me say that integrity is the foundation of public trust. And disclosure is the first step to ethics in government. This proposal increases our disclosure of sources of income, of any relationships we might have with the private sector. Once adopted, it will put behind us this whole notion that you have to be a friend of a friend or a crony to do business with the City. In my opinion, that's never been true; but there is widespread belief of that throughout our City.

One of my favorite stories—and you're going to think I'm telling one—occurred when I was leafleting about a year before the campaign. I was in West End in front of a doughnut shop, standing on the corner in the rain. I handed a brochure—which was a mimeographed sheet, not four colors on beautiful paper—to a young man about ten or eleven years old as he was eating a doughnut and walking along. "Young man," I said, "I'm Shirley Franklin and I'm running for mayor." Without looking up he said, "We need a new mayor." He didn't care who I was, and didn't look up to find out, but I knew that it was time for a change if a ten-year-old saw the problem.

I realize Atlanta is ready for a new style of leadership and I hope a new ethics code is a start. I am very proud that this was the first piece of discretionary legislation that I proposed to the council. I expect that we will be able to live up to the terms and conditions as proposed, and that we will be successful in recruiting a strong ethics officer who will be known to you and others within city government.

We expect to make great progress in changing the culture of government, and our ethics initiative is the cornerstone of this change. I will not tell you that it is easy. I won't tell you it is automatic. I will tell you that that is the challenge in local government today. And my challenge to you is to hold me, and every elected official, to the highest possible, standard of ethics, transparency, honesty, and truthfulness.

Index

Abercrombie & Fitch, 53
Ability, 75
Academia: and accounting problems, 46; and moral character, 64–70; research vs. perception, 44
Accounting ethical crises, 43–50
Acquisitions, 94
Advancement, 6–7, 92
Advertising: and integrity, 51; in pharmaceutical industry, 60–61; as reflection of consumer, 53
Advocacy organization, 5
Airline business, 74–79
Andersen, Arthur, 45, 50
Annan, Kofi, 11
The Aspect of Love (Webber), 74, 77
Attitude, 75
Auditing ethical crises, 43–50
Authenticity, 90–91
Automobile transportation industry, 97–102

Beyond Entrepreneurship (Collins and Lazier), 90
Board of directors, 73
Board members, 24, 25, 108
Built to Last (Collins and Porras), 98, 103, 105
Business morality, 55
Business Roundtable, 27–28, 29, 32

Buying power, 83

Campaigns, 107–10
Centesimus Annus, 38–39
CEOs: "customers, employees, owners," 33; role of, 73; salary and compensation of, 24, 28–29, 78–79; securing retirement of, 75–76; selecting ethical leaders, 19–20
Change: of corporate image, 19–25; from crisis, 3–11; and governance, 26–34; and leadership challenges, 103–6; and religious ethics, 35–40; and social responsibility, 12–18
Chaplains in workplace, 99, 101
Character and higher education, 64–70
Christian business perspective, 38–40, 98–101
CIP (community internship program), 82–85
Citizenship, 3, 5, 62, 65–66
Civic responsibility. *See* Citizenship
Clients. *See* Customers
Coca-Cola Company, 5, 8–9, 10
Collins, James, 98, 103
Colvard, Mark, 84, 85
Community Internship Program (CIP), 82–85
Community involvement, 22–23, 106

Compensation: of executives, 24, 75–76,
    78–79; performance-based, 28, 29, 34
Competitiveness, 55–63, 78
Confidence. *See* Trust
Consumers. *See* Customers
"Contractual" workplace approach, 37–38,
    40
Cooper, Samuel T., 52
Core values, 86–89, 98–102, 103–6
Corporate governance guidelines, 27,
    29–30
Corporate model, 31–32
Corporate social responsibility (CSR),
    15–16, 62, 106
Corporate trust and ethics, 19–25
Costs: in airline operations, 78; in
    healthcare, 61; of mistakes, 104; of
    prescriptions, 59
"Covenantal" workplace approach,
    38–40
Credit, 104–5
Crises, 25, 43–50. *See also* Litigation;
    Scandals
Curricular requirements, 66–68
Customers: attention to, 88–90; discussing
    values with, 91; informing, 11; knowing,
    76–78; needs of, 52

Daniels, Aubrey, 100
De Pree, Max, 39
Delta, 74–79
Democracy, 66
Dependency resentment, 57–58
Dignity, 8, 9, 37, 40, 74, 81
Discrimination, 7, 37. *See also* Diversity
Diversity: in advertising, 52, 54; in auto
    transportation business, 98; importance
    of, 23; in management, 6, 21, 80–85;
    and religion, 36
Downsizing, 22, 39
Drucker, Peter, 60, 62
Drug discovery, 58–59
Dunlap, Al, 20

Earthlink, 94, 95
Economist, on corporate social
    responsibility, 16

Education: job training, 104; and moral
    character, 64–70. *See also* Academia
Eliot, T.S., 48
Employees: acquisitions, 94; awards and
    recognition, 100; city, 108, 109; hiring,
    92, 103–4; relationship to management,
    99, 101; respect for, 22–23, 86; in
    retirement, 100–101; trust of, 105
Energy demands, 13
Enlightened self-interest, 14, 18, 61
Enron, 45, 50, 74
Environmentalism: and globalization, 4, 5;
    for profit, 16; social expectations of, 13

Fastow, Andy, 74
Feurestein, Aaron, 20
Financial disclosure monitoring, 108
Flexibility, 81, 83, 87
Fraud. *See* Litigation; Scandals
Friedman, Milton, 14

Garrett, Dave, 75
General Education in a Free Society, 65
General Electric, 16
"Generally accepted accounting
    principles," 45–46
Globalization: and corporate citizenship,
    3–11; and religion, 36; trends in, 12–13
Good to Great (Collins), 21, 103
Governance guidelines, 27, 29–30
Government ethics, 107–10
Green Street Properties LLC, 86, 87
Growth. *See* Acquisitions; Energy
    demands; Globalization; Mergers

Healthcare system, 55
Higher education. *See* Academia;
    Education
Hiring, 92, 103–4
Homebuilding market, 103–6
Human capital strategy, 84
Human rights, 5, 8–9
Humanity, issues facing, 4

Immelt, Jeff, 16
Institute for Corporate Ethics at the Darden
    School, 32

Integrity, 51–54, 86, 105, 107, 110
Investors. *See* Shareholders
"Invisible hand" doctrine, 14–15, 57
ISP industry, 86–96

Jewish business perspective, 37–38, 40
Jockey International, 51–54
John Wieland Homes, 103–6
Johnson & Johnson, 32–33

Kirkley, Dorothy, 108

Labor negotiations, 97–102
Lane, Mills B., 105
Laws. *See* Legislation
Leadership. *See* Management
Legislation: of Atlanta city ethics, 108–9;
    of business conduct, 24, 25; effect on
    accounting/auditing profession,
    49–50; in response to corporate
    scandal, 28. *See also* Sarbanes-Oxley
    Act
Levitt, Arthur, 47
Literacy, 66–67
Litigation: of auditing firms, 49; conflict of
    interest case, 68–69; and dishonest
    behavior, 24; impact cases, 5; principles
    for facing, 6–10

Malden Mills, 20
Management: accountant and auditors
    against, 47; challenges of, 103–6;
    Christian, 98; diversity in, 80–85; and
    employee relationships, 99, 101;
    promotions, 92; and trust, 78–79; with
    values, 86–96
Margolis, J.D., 33
Market capitalism, 17–18
Market fundamentalism, 4
Market theory, 62
Marketing. *See* Advertising
Menand, Luke, 68
Mencken, H.L., 48
Mergers, 94
Merton, Robert, 30
Miller, Chris, 94
MindSpring, 86–96

Minorities. *See* Discrimination; Diversity
Minority group buying power, 83
Mission statement, at universities, 65
Moses, financial practices of, 35

Natural resources, 4
Nongovernmental organizations (NGOs),
    13

Office Depot, 30, 31, 33–34
O'Malley, Shawn, 47
Operation clockwork, 78
Organized labor agreements, 97–102
Outsourcing, 12, 22, 78

Paine, Lynn Sharp, 56
Paul, Saint, 38
Peale, Norman Vincent, 99
Perception of ethical accounting/auditing,
    44–45
Performance management program, 100
Pfizer Inc., 58, 61
Plato, 65, 69
Political ethics, 107–10
Pope John Paul II, 38
Porras, Jerry, 103
Poverty, 5, 13, 82
Pree, Max De, 39
Prescription spending, 59, 60
Price on entry, 5
Principles of Corporate Governance, 27
Principles of Executive Compensation,
    28
Professors as people, 68–69
Profit with Honor (Yankelovich), 14, 18
Profitability: conflicts with, 94–95; and
    customer service, 90–92; and integrity,
    51–54; vs. integrity, 102; long-term vs.
    short-term, 15, 18, 20, 21, 31
Promotion, 6–7, 92
Public Company Accounting Reform and
    Investor Protection Act, 24, 28, 29, 30,
    32, 73
Public health, 16–17, 36, 52, 58, 60
Public perception: of accounting/auditing
    firms, 46, 49; of pharmaceutical
    industry, 57–63

Reforms. *See* Legislation

Regulations. *See* Legislation

Religious ethics, 35–40, 57, 66, 98–101

"Remember the Business in Business Ethics" (Jennings), 20

Research and Development, 58–59, 105

Research vs. education, 66–70

Restructuring. *See* Downsizing

Risk, managing, 30–31

Rousseau, Jean Jacques, 32

Russell, 19, 21–22, 23

Safety, 74–75, 76

Saint Paul, 38

Sarbanes-Oxley Act, 24, 28, 29, 30, 32, 73

Sayre, Wallace, 64

Scandals: effect on business community, 26, 28, 32, 76; Enron, 45, 50, 74; ethics breakdown, 43–44; Wall Street insider trading, 24

Scott, Lee, 16

Sex sells, 51–52

Shareholder value, 5, 15, 28, 30, 31, 94–95

Shareholders: communications, 29–30; and core value philosophy, 94–95; and invisible hand doctrine, 14–15; and social responsibility, 84; as sole stakeholder, 20, 62; as traders, 31

Shleifer, Andrei, 68–69

Simpler fares, 77–78

Smith, Adam, 14, 57

Social responsibility: citizenship as, 3; corporate, 15–16, 62, 106; and diversity in leadership, 81; and ethical standards, 44; investors and, 84; as a result of CIP training, 83; to students, 64–70

Strategic dialogue, 17, 18

Strikes, 99

Student freedom, 66–67

Students. *See* Academia; Education

Summers, Larry, 3

Supervisors. *See* CEOs; Management

Teachers as people, 68–69

Teamsters union, 97–102

Technology and globalization, 4

Texaco, 7

Thompson, Larry, 32

Training, 104

Transparency, 13, 15, 29, 33, 74

Transportation industry, 80–85, 97–102

Trends affecting business, 12–13, 17–18

Trimble, Joan, 105–6

Trust: as basis of competition, 56; building, 73–79; and campaigns, 107, 110; effect of scandals on, 26, 76; in employees, 105; in pharmaceutical industry, 57–58, 59–63; restoring, 19–25

Trust equity, 14, 18

Union workforce, 97–102

United Parcel Service (UPS), 80–85

Values-based leadership, 86–96

Wal-Mart, 16

Watson, Tom, 15–16

Watson Wyatt 2002 Capital Index Study, 84

Whitley, Matthew, 10

Women, 37, 81

WorldCom, 74

About the Editor and Contributors

EDITOR

JOHN C. KNAPP is founder, professor, and director of The Southern Institute for Business and Professional Ethics at Georgia State University's J. Mack Robinson College of Business. He also is an adjunct professor of ethics at Columbia Theological Seminary, where he teaches courses in ethics and economic life, and a visiting lecturer at the University of Wales, Lampeter. Known internationally as an expert in ethics and leadership, his work to promote understanding of ethics was recognized with the 2001 Georgia Governor's Award in the Humanities and in with his 2007 induction into the Martin Luther King, Jr., International Collegium of Scholars at Morehouse College. Prior to joining the faculty of Georgia State University, he was senior scholar and professor of ethical leadership at Kennesaw State University, where he continues to serve on the advisory board of the Siegel Institute for Leadership, Ethics & Character. He is a director of Atlanta Convention and Visitors Bureau, Georgia Humanities Council, Georgia Committee for Ethical Judicial Campaigns, and Society for Human Resources Management-Atlanta, and serves on the advisory board of the Rutland Institute for Ethics at Clemson University. His most recent book is *For the Common Good: The Ethics of Leadership in the 21st Century* (Praeger, 2007).

CONTRIBUTORS

The following are current biographies of contributors, which reflect any changes in titles and professional affiliations that have occurred since the time their speeches were originally delivered.

CHARLES M. BREWER is chairman of Green Street Properties, LLC, a real estate development company dedicated to the principles of new urbanism and smart growth, including environmentally sound practices in design, construction, and building operation. He is best known as the founder and CEO of MindSpring Enterprises, which grew from thirty-four customers in February 1994 to more than one million. The company completed an initial public offering in 1996, and in 1999 it merged with EarthLink Network to form the second-largest Internet service provider in the nation. He serves on the boards of directors of the Midtown (Atlanta) Alliance, The Commerce Club, and the Atlanta Police Foundation, and on the Board of Councilors of the Carter Center.

JAMES E. COPELAND, JR., retired in 2003 as chief executive officer of Deloitte & Touche in the United States and its global parent, Deloitte Touche Tohmatsu. He currently serves as senior fellow for corporate governance with the U.S. Chamber of Commerce, as a global scholar at Georgia State University's Robinson College of Business, and as a member of the boards of directors for Coca-Cola Enterprises, ConocoPhillips, and Equifax, Inc. He is also a member of the boards of the Woodruff Arts Center in Atlanta, Voices for Georgia's Children, American Friends of the Phelophepa Health Care Train, Georgia Research Alliance. He previously served as an International Councilor of the Center for Strategic and International Studies and on the Board of Directors of The September 11th Fund, the New York City Partnership, and the U.S.-Japan Business Council. He also was a member of the Council of the World Economic Forum, and has been a member of the Society of International Business Fellows since 1983.

CAL DARDEN retired in 2005 as senior vice president for U.S. operations at United Parcel Service. In this position he was accountable for 320,000 employees and $24 billion in revenues. A native of Buffalo, New York, he was a college student when he joined UPS as a part-time package handler and was promoted to positions of increasing responsibility across the nation. Prior to assuming responsibility for the entire United States, he was responsible for one-half of the U.S. operations. Before that, he was UPS's first Corporate Strategic Quality Coordinator and developed the company's quality strategy, focusing on customer satisfaction, employee empowerment, process improvement, and effective methods of measurement. He has served on the board of directors of the National Urban League and has been actively involved in 100 Black Men of North Metro Atlanta, United Way, and his church. While active in corporate leadership, he was ranked eighth on *Fortune*'s listing of 50 Most Powerful Black Executives in America.

SHIRLEY FRANKLIN was elected mayor of the city of Atlanta in 2001. A first-time candidate for public office, she became the first female mayor of Atlanta and the first African American woman to serve as mayor of a major southern city. *Governing* magazine named her 2004 Public Official of the Year; *Time* magazine has named her one of the top five mayors in the country; and U.S. News and World Report and the Center for Public Leadership at Harvard University's Kennedy School of Government have recognized her as one of "America's Best Leaders."

She is a recipient of the 2005 John F. Kennedy Profile in Courage Award and the 2006 Ethics Advocate Award of The Southern Institute for Business and Professional Ethics at Georgia State University. She is president of Georgia Municipal Association, chair of the U.S. Conference of Mayors' Women's Caucus, and president of the National Conference of Democratic Mayors. Earlier in her career, she served in Atlanta city government as commissioner of Cultural Affairs, chief administrative officer, and city manager. She also served as senior vice president for external relations for the Atlanta Committee for the Olympic Games.

GERALD GRINSTEIN was named chief executive officer of Delta Air Lines in January 2004. He has been a director of Delta Air Lines since 1987 and served as Delta's nonexecutive chairman from August 1997 to October 1999, chairing the board's executive sessions thereafter. He served as nonexecutive chairman of Agilent Technologies from 1999 through November 2002. He retired as chairman and CEO of Burlington Northern Inc. in 1995 after overseeing the company's acquisition of Santa Fe Pacific Corp., which created the nation's largest railroad. He was elected to the board of directors of BNI in 1985; was named vice chairman in 1987; president and CEO in 1989; chairman, president, and CEO in 1990; and chairman and CEO in 1991. Before joining BNI, he was president and chief operating officer of Western Airlines Inc., from 1984 to 1985, and CEO of Western from 1985 to March 1987, when Western merged with Delta. Earlier, he was a partner in the law firm of Preston, Thorgrimson, Ellis & Holman in Seattle from 1969 to 1983. His prior career includes serving as chief counsel to the U.S. Senate Commerce Committee, counsel to the Merchant Marine & Transportation Subcommittee, and administrative assistant to U.S. Senator Warren G. Magnuson. He is a trustee of the Henry M. Jackson Foundation and a trustee of the University of Washington Foundation.

KAREN KATEN is retired vice chairman of Pfizer, the world's largest pharmaceutical company; and she is chairman of the Pfizer Foundation, the company's global philanthropic arm devoted to supporting healthcare access, education, and community outreach initiatives. Most recently, she served as president of Pfizer Human Health—the company's principal operating group, responsible for discovery, development, manufacture, distribution, and commercialization of prescription medicines, and for providing a broad array of innovative human-health services. She serves as a trustee at the University of Chicago and a council member of its Graduate School of Business. A director on the boards of General Motors, Harris, RAND, Catalyst and the Economic Club of New York, she has also served a wide variety of healthcare-related enterprises—including PhRMA, the National Alliance for Hispanic Health and the Healthcare Leadership Council—and various international policy bodies, including the U.S.-Japan Business Council, where she is the outgoing chair. She was named among the top ten in *Fortune* Magazine's ranking of "50 Most Powerful Women in Business" in 2005, a list that included her for eight consecutive years.

HARRY R. LEWIS is Gordon McKay Professor of Computer Science at Harvard University, where he was dean of Harvard College from 1995 to 2003. As dean, he oversaw the undergraduate experience, including residential life, career services, public service, academic and personal advising, athletics, and intercultural and race relations. He is a long time member of the College's Admissions Committee. His most recent book is *Excellence Without a Soul: How a Great University Forgot Education.* A member of the Harvard Faculty since 1974, he was honored in 2003 with the title of Harvard College Professor in recognition of his teaching excellence. He is the author of five books and numerous articles on various aspects of computer science. Graduating from Harvard College in 1968, he served for two years as a commissioned officer of the United States Public Health Service. After a year in Europe as a Traveling Fellow of Harvard University, he returned to Harvard in 1971 to complete his Ph.D. He joined the Harvard faculty in the fall of 1974.

STEVE ODLAND joined Office Depot as chairman and chief executive officer in March 2005. Prior to joining Office Depot, he was chairman, chief executive officer, and president of AutoZone, the nation's largest auto parts and accessories retailer, which he joined in 2001. In 2004, AutoZone had over $5.6 billion in net sales, and approximately 3,500 stores and 45,000 employees across the United States and Mexico. Previously, he was chief operating officer of Ahold USA, Inc., a leading supermarket retailer on the eastern seaboard. Prior to that, he served as president and chief executive officer for Tops Markets, Inc., one of Ahold's operating companies. Before joining Ahold, he served as president of the food service division of Sara Lee Corporation and spent sixteen years at The Quaker Oats Company in various senior management capacities. He is also a director of General Mills, Inc. In 2004 he was chairman of the Business Roundtable's Corporate Governance Task Force and was named top new CEO in 2002 by *Bloomberg Markets* magazine.

DEVAL L. PATRICK was elected Governor of the Commonwealth of Massachusetts in November of 2006 and is the first African American to hold the position. Previously he was executive vice president, general counsel, and corporate secretary of The Coca-Cola Company, where he served as part of the company's senior leadership team and its executive committee. Prior to joining The Coca-Cola Company in 2001, he was vice president and general counsel of Texaco, a position he was offered in 1999 after serving for two years as the U.S. District Court-appointed chair of Texaco's Equality and Fairness Task Force. He has practiced law with major private law firms and was appointed by President Clinton in 1994 as Assistant Attorney General for Civil Rights, the nation's top civil rights post. He has served on numerous charitable and corporate boards, as well as the Federal Election Reform Commission under Presidents Carter and Ford, and as vice chair of the Massachusetts Judicial Nominating Council by appointment of Governor Weld.

ROBERT J. RUTLAND is chairman of the board of Allied Holdings Inc., the world's largest transporter of automobiles from manufacturers to dealerships. Listed on the New York Stock Exchange, the company has operations on three continents and handling 65 percent of all new cars in the United States and Canada. He is also chairman of Greyland Real Estate Investments Inc. and in 1997 was named Executive of the Year by the Georgia Securities Association. A director of Fidelity Bank, Atlanta, he has served as chairman of the board of the Department of Natural Resources of the State of Georgia; chairman of the DeKalb Chamber of Commerce; chairman of Georgians for Better Transportation; and a director of Georgia Baptist Health Care Systems. An active supporter of higher education, he has been a trustee of Mercer University and a member of the board of governors of The Southern Institute for Business and Professional Ethics at Georgia State University. Through his commitment to ethics education, he helped establish the Robert J. Rutland Institute for Ethics at Clemson University, his alma mater.

DEBRA S. WALLER is chairman and chief executive officer of Jockey International, a leading apparel manufacturing and marketing company headquartered in Kenosha, Wisconsin, employing over 5,000 people around the world. She joined the company as an administrative assistant in 1982 and has since held positions including director of women's merchandising, vice president/general merchandise manager of Jockey for Her, senior vice president of special markets, executive vice president and assistant to the president. Since January 2001 she has been chairman and chief executive officer following in the steps of her mother, Donna Wolf Steigerwaldt, who had previously held this post in the family-owned business. She serves on the boards of directors of Church Mutual Life Insurance, Marshall & Ilsley Bank, and the Dave Thomas Foundation for Adoption. A trustee of Carthage College, she has long been a leader in the apparel industry where she has served on the Intimate Apparel Council and the sales and marketing committee of the American Apparel & Footwear Association. She also has served as a member of advisory board of the Yale Center for Faith and Culture.

JOHN F. WARD served as chairman and chief executive officer of Russell Corporation, a $1.4 billion international sporting goods company, from April 1998 until August 2006. He began his career with Proctor & Gamble and H. J. Heinz and joined the L'eggs division of Hanes Corporation in 1972. In 1992 he was appointed senior vice president of Sara Lee Corporation, the acquirer of Hanes Corporation, and named chief executive officer of the multibillion-dollar Hanes Group of companies in 1993. In 1996, Ward became president of the J. F. Ward Group and was an executive-in-residence at Wake Forest University's Calloway School of Business and Accounting, where he taught ethics. He has served on a number of boards of directors for public companies and private corporations and is a past chairman of the American Apparel and Footwear Association. In 2004 he was one of ten national business leaders recognized by Diversity Best Practices and Women's Network for his outstanding commitment to diversity. A frequent speaker on ethics, diversity, and corporate responsibility, he currently serves as executive-in-residence at The Southern Institute for Business and Professional Ethics at Georgia State University's J. Mack Robinson College of Business.

JOHN WIELAND is founder, chairman, and chief creative officer of John Wieland Homes and Neighborhoods, the Southeast's leading builder of semicustom homes, with more than 1,000 full-time employees. In his first year in the home building industry he built twenty homes. Now more than three decades and 25,000 homes later, the company builds in Georgia, South Carolina, and Tennesee. *Professional Builder* magazine has named him National Builder of the Year, and the company has received the National Housing Quality Award of the National Association of Home Builders Research Center. In 2006, he was named the Council for Quality Growth's Four Pillar Honoree for contributions to the growth, economic development, and quality of life in the Atlanta region. He is a former chairman of the board of directors of the Federal Reserve Bank of Atlanta and is the immediate past chair of the advisory council for the Emory University Center for Ethics. He has served on the boards of the High Museum of Art; the Hirshhorn Museum and Sculpture Garden of the Smithsonian Institution; the Piedmont Hospital Foundation, the Fund for Theological Education; and the Metro Atlanta Chamber of Commerce.

DANIEL YANKELOVICH has spent a half century monitoring social change and public opinion in America and is author of 2006 book *Profit with Honor: The New Stage of Market Capitalism.* In the 1960s he founded and developed the well-known market research firm of Yankelovich, Skelly and White. In the 1970s and 1980s he initiated the *New York Times*/Yankelovich poll; founded (with Cyrus Vance) Public Agenda, a nonpartisan and not-for-profit public policy research organization; and established DYG Inc., a firm that tracks social and market trends. In the 1990s he founded his newest firm, Viewpoint Learning, which specializes in dialogue-based learning. He is director *emeritus* of companies including CBS, US West, and Loral Space and Communications, and has been a trustee of Brown University, the Kettering Foundation, the Fund for the City of New York, and the Educational Testing Service. A member of the American Academy of Arts and Sciences and the Council on Foreign Relations, and he has affiliations with a number of leading universities including University of California, San Diego, where he recently endowed the Yankelovich Chair in Social Thought. He has authored eleven books.

EDWARD ZINBARG retired in 1994 as executive vice president of Prudential Insurance Company. During almost thirty-five years of service, he was chief economist, chief investment officer for publicly traded securities, and chief administrative officer. He was adjunct professor of finance at City University of New York for fifteen years, and coauthored *Investment Analysis and Portfolio Management* (Richard D. Irwin), a widely used textbook that appeared in five editions over a twenty-year period. His most recent book is *Faith, Morals and Money: What the World's Religions Tell Us about Ethics in the Marketplace.* He has served as a director of the Merrill Lynch mutual fund complex and a major private trust fund; as president of Oheb Shalom Congregation (South Orange, New Jersey); and on the boards of a number of religious, philanthropic, and cultural institutions including the Rabbinical School of The Jewish Theological Seminary, the New Jersey Symphony Orchestra, the National Ramah Commission (of Jewish summer camping), and the Jewish Community Foundation of MetroWest.